Counseling
and
Children

RESOURCES FOR
CHRISTIAN COUNSELING

VOLUME TWENTY-TWO

Counseling and Children

WALTER BYRD, M.D.
PAUL WARREN, M.D.

RESOURCES FOR CHRISTIAN COUNSELING

General Editor

Gary R. Collins, Ph.D.

WORD PUBLISHING

Dallas · London · Sydney · Singapore

Unless otherwise identified, quotations from the Bible in this volume are taken from the New American Standard Bible, © 1960, 1962, 1963, 1968, 1971, 1972, 1973, 1975, 1977 by the Lockman Foundation. Used by permission. Those identified KJV are from the King James Version.

Library of Congress Cataloging-in-Publication Data

Byrd, Walter, 1949–
    Counseling and children / Walter Byrd and Paul Warren.
      p. cm. — (Resources for Christian counseling ; v. 22)
    Includes bibliographical references.
    ISBN 0-8499-0597-4
    1. Church work with children. 2. Children—Pastoral counseling
of. 3. Church work with families. 4. Family—Religious life.
I. Warren, Paul, 1949–   II. Title. III. Series.
BV639.C4B97   1989
253.5'2—dc20   89-39921
                                          CIP

Printed in the United States of America

4 5 6 7 8 9 9 AGF 9 8 7 6 5 4 3

CONTENTS

EDITOR'S PREFACE

I HAD READ ABOUT IT FOR YEARS and wondered, on occasion, how my wife and I would react when it was our turn. How would we handle the empty nest? What would our house be like without the kids?

For almost twenty-three years we had at least one of our daughters living at home. After the birth of each, we committed each one to the Lord and determined to be good parents. At times we failed, like all parents, and so often we seemed to have no idea how to handle crises. But we prayed diligently, sometimes talked to other parents or consulted books, determined to make the best decisions possible, and with God's help over the years were able to build good rapport within our little family. For over two decades our house and our lives were filled with activity and sometimes with hordes of young friends.

Then they went to college—both of them in the same year. We discovered the truth in the old adage:

It is easier to give your kids roots than to give them wings.

We tried not to push them out but we tried not to hold them either. As we watched them grow into adulthood, we learned to loosen our grip on the reins, even when we wondered if they were mature enough or experienced enough to make it on their own.

And now they are gone. Tears flood my eyes even as I write these words only a few days after the last one departed, as I consider this now-quiet house, their empty rooms, and our sense of loss. No longer can I rescue them or protect them as we did in the past. No longer can I teach them daily to walk in the ways of the Lord—that time for training is gone. Like young eaglets who flutter out of the nest, our girls are learning to fly on their own. And that is as it should be.

They will write often. We talk on the phone and are building even better relationships between family members now that we all are adults. To be honest, we wouldn't really want it any other way.

Even so, the departure of our children has reminded us that sons and daughters are on loan from God. We have them for only a few years and they are gone. They are placed, by an all-wise God, into the hands of inexperienced and sometimes unwise parents who often flounder and frequently make mistakes. Sometimes those children, whom we loved and nourished as little ones, develop learning disabilities, conflicts with peers or with parents, psychological or physical abnormalities, rebellious attitudes, destructive friendships, low self-esteem or a host of other problems. As parents, and as counselors of both parents and children, we need all the help we can get.

In this volume of the Resources for Christian Counseling series, two physicians give us this kind of help. Dr. Walter Byrd is a psychiatrist who has worked with young people for most of his professional career. Dr. Paul Warren is a pediatrician who works mostly with disturbed or struggling children and their parents. Together these Christian doctors give a concise and practical overview of the issues facing children and parents during the stressful times in which we live.

Like all other volumes in the Resources for Christian Counseling series, this book is intended to be practical and helpful. Written by counseling experts, each of whom has a strong Christian commitment and extensive counseling experience, the books are meant to be examples of accurate psychology and careful use of Scripture. Each is intended to have a clear evangelical perspective, careful documentation, a strong practical orientation, and freedom from the sweeping statements and undocumented rhetoric that sometimes characterize writing in the counseling field. Our goal is to provide books that are clearly written, useful, up-to-date overviews of the issues faced by contemporary Christian counselors—including pastoral counselors. All of the Resources for Christian Counseling books have similar bindings and together they are intended to comprise a helpful encyclopedia of Christian counseling.

Walter Byrd coauthored an earlier book in this series; and the present volume, on children, is the first of two that are coauthored with Paul Warren. A later book will consider counseling adolescents and their parents.

It is my hope that these books, drawn from the wide experience of two dedicated and competent counselors, will enable you to help children and their parents to cope with the problems of child-rearing and parent-child relationships.

Some day the children that you see will have left home, the family nests will be empty and for all of us the active days of parenting will be over. By helping parents and their children, you can bring greater family harmony now and a sense of satisfaction and good feelings in the future, when the kids leave and the parents feel the hope, the joy, and the sadness of an empty nest.

Gary R. Collins, Ph.D.
Kildeer, Illinois

INTRODUCTION

THE BIBLE HAS MUCH TO SAY ABOUT CHILDREN. We are told that children are "a gift of the Lord" (Ps. 127:3), that child-rearing is crucial in determining the child's future life course (Prov. 22:6), that teaching biblical precepts is an essential task of parenting (Deut. 6:7), that discipline is an act of parental love (Prov. 19:8, Eph. 6:4), and that Jesus, indeed, loves children (Mark 10:13–16). There can be no doubt that it is God's will that we love and train our children.

Life can be quite difficult for children. The world we live in is increasingly more chaotic, and our children are exposed to that chaos. Conflict, violence, materialism, substance abuse, child abuse, and divorce are but a few of the stresses impacting our children. Coping with these stresses often seems overwhelming even to adults. Our children, whose energies need to be directed toward the necessary steps of physical, emotional, and spiritual growth, are increasingly becoming stymied in their development by the stress that surrounds them.

Over the last several years we, the authors, have discussed the unique opportunities that Christian counselors have to affect the lives of children and their families. God's plan for growing up is an exciting and intricate journey whose every step is crucially important. We feel that in order to effectively minister to children a counselor must be equipped with an understanding of the basic principles of child development. He or she will also need a repertoire of counseling skills to meet the physical and emotional needs of children, and a commitment to understanding the importance of the child's family in solving emotional and behavioral problems.

Furthermore, we believe that it is equally important for the counselor to minister to the child's spiritual needs. The Bible clearly teaches us that we are not only physical and emotional beings but also spiritual beings and that answers to life's problems must address spiritual needs. Herein, we feel, lies the unique opportunity of the pastor and Christian counselor to influence the lives of children whose problems leave them hurting, angry, confused, lonely, and discouraged.

For this reason, we have written *Counseling and Children*. We have sought to offer instruction and encouragement to the Christian counselor whose job it is to minister to the developmental, emotional, and spiritual needs of children. While at times this task is difficult, there is no more important challenge and no more rewarding opportunity for ministry, ". . . for the kingdom of God belongs to such as these" (Mark 10:14b).

PART ONE

THE YOUNG CHILD

CHAPTER ONE

WINNING THE CHILD-REARING CONTEST

REARING A CHILD IS LIKE A CONTEST—a contest in which the stakes are high because they involve the healthy development of the child's personality. The "contestants" are the parents, who strive to help the child mature properly, and the child, who often perceives the child-rearing process as a challenge to his or her own self-expression.

If the parent does not rise to the occasion and "parent" the child, then the child grows up with an insecure, undisciplined, and often maldeveloped self-concept. On the other hand, if the child is overwhelmed and coerced into an unnatural capitulation, then the child never fully develops as an individual. Again, the outcome is not favorable.

More than ever, Christian counselors are called upon to help parents and children with the ground rules of this contest. Therefore, this book is designed to be a game plan as the counselor (and the parent) helps children between birth and age eleven with the process of growing into healthy maturity.

These chapters will consolidate, organize, and present information counselors and parents will find invaluable as a child's personality develops through the various stages of his or her life.

The counselor often is asked to help parents attain the balance between too much control and too much flexibility. This book will offer ways in which the child can develop individuality as well as responsibility and, in time, the capacity to relate to others on a mature basis.

STAGES OF DEVELOPMENT

To understand and work with children, we first must identify the two major stages of a child's development. Stage 1, the young child, represents ages birth through six. Stage 2, the grade-school child, represents ages seven through eleven.

In each of these stages, the parent's responsibilities differ. Therefore, any counselor helping a child or a family with a problem should remember these stages and how both the parent's tasks and the child's personality configurations change in each stage.

During young childhood, ages birth through six, the parent's main responsibilities are *containing* and *framing.* Containing involves providing the child's basic needs, enabling the child to feel safe, secure, and accepted. Framing involves providing the basic foundational elements of the child's personality structure.

The "framing in" of the child's personality during the first six years of life is similar to the "framing in" process which occurs when a house is built. The foundation is laid; then the house is framed according to the builder's design. This "framing in" will determine the house's shape and functional nature. So, too, the "framing in" of the child's personality during the first six years of life will determine to a great extent the eventual temperament, personality style, and self-concept of the later developmental years, including adulthood.

4

During the grade-school stage, ages seven through eleven, the parent's main responsibilities are *training* and *engaging*. In the training years, the child involves himself or herself in the school process and in learning tremendous amounts of practical information which form the basis of virtually all future education. The child develops a distinctly individual personality during these years. Spiritual training also is a crucial element of this grade-school period.

The engaging process that occurs during these years sees the child involved in interpersonal relationships in a major way. In these years, the child forms same-sex friendships and crystallizes a sense of fair play and a belief in the rules of society. The child also develops an understanding of the innate existence of right and wrong.

During these years, a child begins to utilize his or her particular type of intelligence and becomes comfortable solving problems and navigating through life's maze. Dr. Robert Sternberg of Yale University has proposed three types of intelligence: componential, experiential, and contextual. *Componential* is analytical thinking, usually resulting in high scores in test-taking and in analytical problem-solving. *Experiential* intelligence involves creative thinking and seeing how to combine seemingly unrelated experiences in insightful ways to solve problems. The *contextual* thinker is strong in the area of common sense. He or she is "street smart" and knows how to survive and negotiate in terms of relevant variables and key relationships.[1]

GAME-PLAN COMPONENTS

To assist the child, we propose the "N.O.W." game plan. In this acronym, "N" stands for needs, "O" stands for options, and "W" stands for ways for change.

In understanding the shaping of behavior and character of the child, a parent or counselor must address these three areas in every significant situation. The child's needs in a particular situation, the child's options in a particular situation, and the ways for change (or, changeable behaviors and attitudes) must be identified and dealt with in order to help guide the child through each circumstance.

5

N.O.W. provides a guideline for counseling and parenting. Ideally, the elements of N.O.W. can be used to develop a successful approach to helping the child. The following chapters will examine needs, options, and ways for change as they contribute to successful counseling and parenting.

Four Overarching Needs

The child continually experiences four overarching needs during the period of birth through age eleven.

1. *Example.* Children most often react in ways that have been modeled by their parents' behavior. These models can be negative or positive.

The boy and girl—each five years old—were playing "house." The girl, a pastor's daughter, began chiding the boy, who sat in a recliner "reading" the newspaper. Obviously parroting a conversation she had heard between her parents many times, the girl said, "Dear, you mustn't stay up too late, now. You want to be fresh for your sermon tomorrow."

The youngster was demonstrating how she had integrated into her personality a basic need of the young child—the need for an example.

2. *Attention.* Parental involvement or attention is crucial to healthy personality development. No substitute exists for the time and interest a parent shows during a child's formative years. As issues surface in therapy, the Christian counselor often will identify factors relating to the positive or negative attention the child is receiving. The counselor often will target these as issues needing to be addressed.

3. *Support.* The parent's positive endorsement of a child's interests and activities is crucial in the parenting process. As the counselor helps the child and parent grow in this area, the parent's mere *acceptance* of the child frequently is not sufficient. The child must *feel* that the parent actively takes initiative to support and endorse the child's healthy interests and pursuits.

4. *Affection.* Most parents would state categorically that they love their children. But children cannot survive emotionally on good intentions or on factual statements about love. Parents must show affection—by holding the child, talking lovingly to the child, appropriately touching the child, smiling at

the child, and speaking to the child in an accepting and compassionate tone. Christian counselors can make a major contribution by helping families show affection effectively, especially now, when multiple priorities place unusual stress on relationships.

A Child's Options

Once the counselor and parent comprehend the child's needs, the next step is understanding the options the child feels he or she has. The Christian counselor and parent should go through the following checklist to identify the child's apparent behavior.

1. *Physical.* Excessive fatigue, hormonal changes, hypoglycemia, food or inhalant allergies, thyroid disorders, or sexual hormone changes can prevent the child from adapting to situations in a healthy way.

2. *Temperamental.* At least nine characteristics distinguish each child's temperament. These include activity level, rhythmicity, approach or withdrawal, adaptability, sensory threshold, quality of mood, intensity of reaction, distractibility, and attention span and persistence.[2] By rhythmicity is meant the predictability within a day's time of the occurrence of natural phenomena such as sleeping and eating. "Approach or withdrawal" is the child's tendency to seek attachment to or separation from other people.

3. *Psychological.* Intrapersonal factors (pertaining to the child's self-concept and self-worth) and interpersonal factors (pertaining to the child's peer relationships and relationships with adults and other family members) affect a child's behavior at any age.

4. *Misinformational.* Misbehavior sometimes occurs as a result of misinformation, when children do not understand their parents' expectations and goals for them or are unable to express their intentions clearly. This misinformation can contribute to a parent-child breakdown in communication in either of the two main developmental stages. (This is an issue that is also of primary importance in the teen years; see *Counseling and the Adolescent,* another volume in this series by the same authors.)

5. *Emotional.* Each child requires a certain amount of emotional involvement with the parent. Dr. Ross Campbell refers to this as the child's "emotional tank."[3] This "tank" remains full

most of the time if the parent gives reasonable attention to the child. Misbehavior sometimes occurs when this "tank" is not relatively full. When a child's emotional tank is underfilled, he or she may begin to "act out" in ways that cause others to become involved. This "acting out" may simply be irritating or attention-seeking behavior or it may progress to outright rebellion and confrontation, representing the child's outcry for parental attention as a way of confirming that the parent cares for the child. As a result of the "acting out," the child's emotional tank is (hopefully) refilled, but not necessarily in an optimally healthy way.

6. *Dissidence* (disobedience). The willful rejection of parental authority is an option open to the child and at times may be the core problem. Once the other options are ruled out as possible explanations for the child's disruptive behavior, then willful disobedience may be the cause. Setting reasonable limits and enforcing those limits, either by consequences or spankings (depending on the child's age and situation), are crucial in helping the child develop responsible behavior within the limits set by authority figures. When a child learns that parents condone and accept disobedience, he or she later will have trouble learning that disobedience is self-destructive in society, at work, in the church, or at home.

Ways for Change

Once the counselor has assessed the child's needs and behavioral options, then he or she can help establish ways for change, action plans that parents, teachers, and others who work with children can use as guidelines. We suggest that these ways can be categorized in the following manner:
1. Limits
2. Consequences
3. Goals
4. Assignments
5. Responsibilities

Although certainly all the action plans that the counselor will develop with the family and/or child will not be this comprehensive, here is a seven-step format for an action plan designed to assist a child in achieving positive ways for change.

Step 1   State (write out) clearly the overall goal—the problem to be solved.

_____

_____

Step 2   What resources (abilities, intelligence, maturity, etc.) are available to the child for solving the problem?

_____

_____

Step 3   What resources does the parent(s) or counselor have to bring to bear on the problem?

_____

_____

Step 4   Plan the specific parent and/or counselor interventions with the child (including rewards and consequences).

_____

_____

Step 5   Establish a timetable for when to start the process, when to evaluate it, how to assure consistency, and approximately how long the action plan will be in duration.

_____

_____

Step 6   Specify how you will know when the goal has been accomplished (i.e., by what criteria can you measure your success?).

_____

_____

Step 7   How can you best plan to prevent a relapse into undesirable behavior(s)?

_____

_____

The chapters that follow will show how the Christian counselor can use the N.O.W. approach, employing these ways for
change to help children to mature properly.

CHAPTER TWO

NEEDS OF THE YOUNG CHILD

ALTHOUGH EMOTIONAL NEEDS undoubtedly exist throughout all ages of the child-rearing process, they are crucially important during the first six years of life. That is the time when we believe that many of the foundations of the child's personality are laid. During this time, each child's personality passes through various stages in an amazingly orderly fashion, according to Erik Erikson's writings about personal psychological development.[1]

In this chapter, we will discuss three psychological "milestones" the child should have achieved by the time he or she turns seven. Then we will consider the need for example and three other emotional needs of the young child.

MILESTONE NO. 1:
BASIC TRUST VS. INSECURITY

In the first six years of life, the child struggles initially with the issue of basic trust versus insecurity. A stable, predictable environment in which explanation always precedes change and where stability surrounds the child like a warm blanket is crucial.

From birth, the child begins to learn that he or she can trust relationships to meet needs, such as being fed, changed, held, or cuddled. If needs are not met, the child will learn that relationships cannot be trusted and that others must be "beaten" to obtain from them needed elements for survival.

Numerous times in counseling, we encounter children who are described as the neighborhood or school "toughs." They are bullies who repeatedly push others around and who use physical prowess to control others, especially younger students. Almost without exception, we discover that the "toughs" are victims of child neglect. These young people learned they could not trust people to meet their needs, so they began pushing others around to get the attention they craved.

Placing a child outside the home for extensive periods, long absences by either mother or father, the death of a parent, the birth of a sibling, or any other event altering the predictability and/or consistency of the social fabric in the young child's home can cause stress.

Naturally, stress is not always bad. Small amounts actually may help the child develop self-independence. But in these years, the child's key struggle initially is for trust and belief in the security of parents and the surrounding world. According to Erikson, the young child's struggle for trust occurs primarily in the first two years but certainly continues through the first decade of life.

MILESTONE NO. 2:
SELF-CONTROL VS. SELF-DOUBT

From ages two through four, the child deals with the inner problem of wanting to be autonomous—in control of his or her own world—versus the difficulty of self-doubt. At this age children not only are literally learning to stand on their own two feet; they are also experimenting with self-control, such as toilet training. They also experiment with ways to gain some measure of control of the environment, through such means as temper tantrums, anger, and "I won't" behaviors.

During this stage, the parent must maintain an uneasy balance between correcting the child (teaching how to respect limits) while at the same time encouraging the child to develop a "free spirit" which supports a sense of self-mastery and self-confidence.

Parents, at first, feel great pride when they see their infant begin to climb up on furniture and scale chair legs, yet they gasp a few minutes later when such adventures cause tumbles. They want the youngster to know the limits of what's safe and what's not, yet they hesitate to discourage forays of independence. The parents, of course, can accomplish both tasks as long as they do so in an environment of predictable love and acceptance.

Between two and four, the child strongly needs to feel the parents are giving unconditional love. The child must know the parents love, accept, and approve of him or her without regard to performance.

MILESTONE NO. 3:
INITIATIVE VS. GUILT AND EMBARRASSMENT

Toward the end of the early childhood period, children will show they need to demonstrate initiative; yet they will feel guilty over mistakes made.

Often, five- and six-year-olds will be too loud or will express themselves with dramatic gestures and creative arguments to get their own way.

Youngsters create fantasy worlds filled with soldiers, wild animals, farms, battlefields, and galaxies in which they carry out their exploits. Or, they dress up in exaggerated costumes, parent imaginary families, and have endless episodes of people achieving and doing great things. As outlandish as some of these exploits may seem, children are sensitive to feeling guilty and foolish if adults see their play activities as frivolous or

13

obnoxious. During this stage, large doses of criticism may foster a prolonged sense of self-ridicule in children. It is our clinical experience that a habit of self-ridicule as a child frequently contributes to a sense of inferiority and fragile self-confidence as an adult.

A six-year-old wants to feel she's grown up enough to walk to school two blocks away; yet she feels horribly embarrassed when she temporarily takes the wrong turn. If her parents rebuke her for her temporary error instead of dealing with her mistake with love and concern, it could scar her for years.

THE FOUR BASIC NEEDS

As mentioned earlier, the young child has four basic needs, including the need for an example.

Example

The phrase "monkey see, monkey do" probably describes the most observable principle in parenting the early child, since the child patterns most of his or her actions after perceptions of how the parents act. Children watch their parents incessantly. They continually observe not only what the parents say, but also the nonverbal cues—how a parent accepts them, a parent's approach to other people, including the spouse and siblings, and a parent's demonstrated priorities in life.

A two-year-old child already knows what is or is not important to his or her parents and can predict with astounding accuracy the parents' reaction to a wide range of situations. A recently reported study in *Science News* showed that fourteen-day-old infants significantly mimicked behaviors they had seen an adult perform one week previously. In a recent study at the University of Washington in Seattle, it was concluded that infants can internalize and remember the acts they see adults perform and can use these memories to guide their own subsequent behavior, even after an interval of time.[2]

Key parental reactions and behaviors lay a foundation for the child's own internal behavior and value system. The child needs the parent not only to demonstrate patience and consistency but also to initiate situations where the parent can observe these qualities in the child. Some parents demonstrate well but don't initiate enough. Other parents initiate regularly but don't follow through by demonstrating patience and consistency with the child. A counselor should stress that parents need not only to model good traits but also to prompt situations that cause the three major milestones to occur.

A husband and wife whose business caused them to dine out with company regularly were concerned that their five-year-old girl learn acceptable table manners. About once a month, one of the parents took the child out to dinner to "practice" good table manners. She learned as much from watching her dad or mom cut meat with a knife and fork and use a napkin as she did from their instructions.

Attention

Parental attention is crucial to the child's development of a healthy personality. The amount of time a parent spends with the child and the degree of interest the parent shows the child during his or her formative years is critical to the maturity process.

Attention is not simply a well-meaning parent's passive acknowledgment of the child. Rather, by "attention" we mean that the parent intentionally sets aside blocks of time to make sure the child knows he or she is important. For this reason, a parent's (or a child's) extensive absence from the home can be risky for the child's emotional health.

Degree of interest shown the child also is important. For example, a parent who knows the child is fascinated with dinosaurs can make special trips to the library to check out books on the subject; or the parent can take the child to the science museum for the new dinosaur exhibit. Children never forget such parental demonstrations of interest.

A senior executive in a large corporation was seen sobbing with emotion when he remembered the first time his father showed him how to change a bicycle tire. A female client once told her counselor of a coloring book page she kept in a special memory box. The page represented the time her father first showed her how to use a tissue to shade crayon marks.

Such memories go all the way to the core of the personality and are indispensable to laying a sound cornerstone in a child's emotional development.

Affection

"I love yous" are necessary, but they are not the be-all and end-all in showing affection to a child. Affection is conveyed in that soft look in the eye, that spontaneous smile when the child catches the parent looking his or her way, and that gentle touch when the child is merely going about his or her own business. Small shows of affection continually throughout the day are much more effective than is a single hug, kiss, and "goodnight, I love you" at bedtime.

Displays of affection are like emotional "breathing" to a child's personality. Lungs, no matter how healthy, must breathe more than once a day in order to continue to function. In like manner, a child cannot survive on a single daily show of affection, no matter how genuine or intense that show may be.

In treating people for depression, psychiatrists often find troubled clients who can never remember a parent saying, "I love you." Research shows that this lack of affection can cause great psychological damage. Lack of father-to-son intimacy and acceptance is emerging as a key factor preventing young males from bonding with the same-sex parent. This gender-identity disorder shows a strong link with later homosexual arousal, according to a fifteen-year study reported at the 1988 convention of the American Psychiatric Association.[3]

When children see that their parents' marriage is healthy, they get the message: "The most important relationship in the family is between mother and father, and this relationship is solid." When that message is received, the child has a greater chance of adjusting confidently to his or her own gender-identity. The young boy must know that "being a boy is just fine," and the young girl must know that "being a girl is just fine." Believing in the confident security of one's own gender-identity is crucial.

Support

A child needs a parent to endorse positively the child's interests and activities. In today's society, parents often overlook this element of the parenting process. One busy father, who repeatedly missed his son's soccer games, excused his absences by telling the soccer coach, "My child knows I'm for him and behind him 100 percent. I don't feel like I have to be here for his matches."

But children don't just "know" any such thing. The soccer-playing child's sad face week after week was evidence that children need to be shown. The counselor must help parents show children their support, which should come when parents act as both encouragers and as fellow participants.

The child not only must feel the parent approves of what he or she does but also that the parent actively endorses the child's healthy interests and pursuits. Support and encouragement lay a foundation for a basic sense of self-acceptance, and self-acceptance forms a basis for healthy self-love. Healthy self-love is crucial not only to the personality but also to the development of appropriate interpersonal relationships.

People who hate themselves eventually develop bitterness and hatefulness toward others. Unfortunately, these patterns often are begun in childhood and only intensify through the adult years. A counselor who helps a struggling family at this juncture in the child's development can not only improve the quality of life for the present family but also for those children in their adult years, in their future families, and in their children's children.

The first six years of life represent an exciting time for the child and a challenging one for the parents. A skillful counselor will help parents see the progression going on within the child during this time. Children initially see themselves as the center of the universe, often needing constant attention. They often feel entitled to their own ways and that they are exempt from rules. At the same time, however, they believe they cause everything bad that happens in their world. This can be an uneasy paradox for young children because it is part of the struggle to establish their own identities and to understand their limits at controlling the world around them.

During this time, children are beginning to see themselves as citizens of the world. Learning to negotiate the intricacies of relationships—with parents as well as with siblings and later with others—occurs in the first six years of life. A counselor's helpful intervention during these years of development can pay rich dividends for the present and the future.

CHAPTER THREE

OPTIONS OF THE YOUNG CHILD

THE THREE-YEAR-OLD BOY SAT ON THE BEACH working industriously on his "tower" of sand. Tugging on his mother's beach towel, he said loudly, "Mommy, come see what I built." But his mother merely nodded in his direction and never left her sunbathing.

The youngster spent the next few minutes kicking his inflatable beach ball. Again he tugged on his mother's towel and said, "Mommy, watch me kick." But the mother merely murmured, "That's nice, honey," and continued her sunning.

The youngster walked away for a minute and returned with his swimsuit pulled down around his ankles. "Now, Mommy, will you watch me?" he said. One way or the other, children will proceed to meet their needs in life.

Like the youngster on the beach, however, the way in which children's needs are met can be either positive or negative in outcome.

A counselor's goal, after determining the child's needs as discussed in chapter 2, is to help the child tip the scale toward using positive options and to minimize the negative side of the balance sheet. Again, as with the child on the beach, the parent has a role in determining which option the child chooses.

In chapter 1, we identified the young child's six options as physical, temperamental, psychological, misinformational, emotional, and disobedient. In this chapter, we will take a closer look at these options and explain how counselors can help parents make sure these positive ones are chosen.

OPTION NO. 1—PHYSICAL

Excessive fatigue, hormonal changes, and physical changes such as hypoglycemia, thyroid disorders, allergies, and hearing and sight difficulties can affect the child's ability to adapt to situations in a healthy manner. Major caregivers such as parents, teachers, baby-sitters, and child-care workers usually notice symptoms of these physical problems, although occasionally some of these problems go undetected. When evaluating a child's misbehavior, an astute counselor or parent will first be certain that none of these conditions exist.

However, a child's emotional state most often is affected by how fatigued he or she is, or how much the child has been stimulated, or how well the child has eaten that day. A physically exhausted child can pose a difficult behavioral problem at the end of a long day. In this situation, a parent is better off getting the child to bed early than imposing a series of punishments and consequences.

Likewise, reducing the sugars and stimulants in a child's diet may change what on the surface appears to be an attitude or conduct disturbance.

OPTION NO. 2—TEMPERAMENTAL

Jeff and Darlene eagerly awaited the birth of their first son, Tommy, and the birth process went well for both mother and baby. Tommy fed well at the breast and switched easily to formula. He was a happy and sociable baby. He cooed and enjoyed being around people. Within three to four months, he was sleeping through the night and took regular naps. Jeff and Darlene felt genuinely positive about their parenting task. When their second child, Johnny, was born they were confident about being parents again.

However, parenting Johnny wasn't at all what they expected. For the first year and a half, Johnny did not sleep well through the night. He didn't nap at regular times and cried much of the time he was awake. He shrank from strangers and often resisted being held by anyone but his mother. He pulled back from grandparents when they tried to hold him. He was a fussy baby when feeding, had indigestion and diarrhea on formula, and was a picky eater on solid foods. Jeff and Darlene began to assume they had made drastic mistakes with Johnny and began to consider themselves as "parental failures."

According to a study conducted by two New York psychiatrists, the disparity between rearing Tommy and Johnny was due to temperamental differences, not necessarily because of some fault with Jeff and Darlene. In the study, Stella Chess, professor of child psychiatry at New York University Medical Center, and Alexander Thomas, professor of psychiatry at the same institution, followed 133 children from early infancy through adulthood. They traced these children's patterns in areas such as behavior, eating, and sleeping to determine if they showed innate and inborn differences, regardless of their parenting or the characteristics of their caregivers.

In reviewing the statistics of their research data, Chess and Thomas were able to identify nine major traits that distinguish a child's basic temperament. These temperament traits, it must be remembered, are primarily biologically and genetically determined and, therefore, cannot be significantly changed by parents. These temperament traits along with the parents' teaching and interacting with the child result in the child's ultimate behaviors. While parents cannot change basic temperament traits, they can "match" their parenting and teaching skills to the child's temperament to bring about the desired behaviors. These temperament traits, which were named in chapter 1, are:

1. *Activity level*—the tempo and frequency of general motor activity.

2. *Rhythmicity*—the degree of regularity of the biological functions of sleeping and waking, eating, etc.

3. *Approach or withdrawal*—the initial reaction to any new stimulus.

4. *Adaptability*—the ability of a child to accept new or altered situations.

5. *Intensity of reaction*—the level of response, irrespective of whether it is positive or negative, to a stimulus.

6. *Quality of mood*—the amount of pleasant, joyful, and friendly behavior as contrasted with unpleasant, crying, unfriendly behavior.

7. *Threshold of responsiveness*—the level of extrinsic stimulus that is necessary to evoke a response.

8. *Distractibility*—the level of ability to ignore extraneous stimuli while completing a task.

9. *Attention span and persistence*—the ability to stay on tasks even when there are no extraneous stimuli.

Chess and Thomas concluded that the particular cluster of these temperament traits clearly contributed to a child's behavior. Certain clusters of temperament characteristics may cause a child to be described as an "easy child." Other temperament clusters would cause a child to be described as a "difficult child." Chess said, "It is not a matter of how a child performs on a single trait or behavior quality, but it is the clustering of those traits that gives a true picture of his true temperament."[1]

Stanley Turecki, in his book, *The Difficult Child,* offers clues about how the nine temperamental traits mentioned above could help a parent determine whether a child is "easy" or "difficult."[2]

We have modified these traits somewhat based on our clinical experience and offer them here in a small table (see Figure 3–1). Although this table is not a formal diagnostic instrument, with us it has been useful in various cases, rendering a thumbnail sketch of the child's general temperament disposition.

With each of the nine traits, three descriptions of the child's behavior are shown. A parent can circle one number under each trait, then add the nine numbers. A score of 9 to 14 could reflect a relatively "easy" child. A score of 15 to 21 could reflect a child with mixed "easy" and "difficult" traits; and a score of 22 to 27 would suggest a more "difficult" child.

Parents of an "easy" child may feel unrealistically pleased with themselves for their superior nurturing, which they feel has contributed to the child's "easiness," while parents of a "difficult" child may feel unjustifiably guilty because of their struggles. Neither gloating nor guilt is necessarily appropriate.

Instead, a parent should take a pat on the back when he or she learns to achieve a good "fit" with the child's temperament. This occurs when the parents fully understand the child's temperament and when they adapt to it. In rearing a difficult child, parents must be firm when dealing with disruptively disobedient behavior. They also must be sensitive when helping the child express his or her natural temperament more responsibly.

Parents can feel angry at their child one moment, and yet at the same time sense a competing inner voice which says, "This poor little child needs my help." When parents sense this push-pull struggle, we recommend that they step back emotionally, get a better perspective on the situation, take the child's temperament into account, and plan the most effective intervention.

In his early childhood, Brad, who from birth fit most of the "difficult child" traits, had a short attention span. His preschool teachers complained of his boisterously loud speech and his tendency to interrupt conversations. Teachers and parents imposed consequences and punishments, but none seemed to impact him long-term.

However, when Brad reached late childhood and early adolescence, he suddenly became interested in making good grades. His improved academic record made him eligible for honors classes at school. His new interest in studying improved his ability to concentrate. In his honors classes, other students looked askance at his boisterous behavior. Brad's internal motivation and the positive peer pressure of other students altered certain aspects of this difficult personality and helped him mature.

No. 1   Quality of Mood

1	2	3
Child is usually pleasant and happy.	Undecided. Child shows neither trait more than the other.	Child frequently cries and often has a "cranky" attitude.

No. 2   Adaptability

1	2	3
Child seems to like changes, is quickly comfortable with switching to a new activity.	Undecided. Child shows neither trait more than the other.	Child tends to get angry or "throw a fit" when stopped from continuing an activity.

No. 3   Sensory Threshold

1	2	3
Child quickly "soothes" or responds to touch.	Undecided. Child shows neither trait more than the other.	Child is not particularly cuddly, seems not to "warm up" to touch.

No. 4   Regularity

1	2	3
Child is relatively easy to work into a schedule of bedtime, naps, meals, habits, etc.	Undecided. Child shows neither trait more than the other.	Child tends to be erratic in schedule and is difficult to work into a routine.

No. 5   Reaction Intensity

1	2	3
Child rarely speaks loudly or spontaneously interrupts conversations.	Undecided. Child shows neither trait more than the other.	Child often spontaneously is loud and tends to verbally interrupt in conversations.

No. 6   Distractibility

1	2	3
If asked to do so, the child can pay attention to something he's not particularly interested in.	Undecided. Child shows neither trait more than the other.	Child has a hard time focusing attention on something unless he is really quite interested in it.

No. 7 Activity level

1	2	3
Child is active on occasion, but usually not noticeably so, nor disruptive.	Undecided. Child shows neither trait more than the other.	Child has a lot of "monkey-like" energy and is generally very obviously active.

No. 8 Approach-Withdrawal

1	2	3
Child easily "takes to" new people emotionally; seems to like even strangers when smiled at.	Undecided. Child shows neither trait more than the other.	Child not comfortable with new people; "sticks" to parents; doesn't like unanticipated changes.

No. 9 Stubbornness

1	2	3
Is flexible in changing a decision or adapting to a change of plans.	Undecided. Child shows neither trait more than the other.	Will stick persistently to an idea or a preference, even when parents try hard to persuade the child otherwise.

Figure 3–1
Determining A Child's Temperament

OPTION NO. 3—PSYCHOLOGICAL

Three main psychological factors may make a difference in a child's behavior.

1. Inside-personal factors. These are stresses and conflicts arising from the child's internal struggles with self-identity and self-esteem. An internal sense of failure or guilt can cause extreme stress even in a young child. Such stress may cause the child to adopt negative options such as disrespectful, excessively childish, and irresponsible behaviors to help him or her solve problems.

2. Outside-personal factors. Influences of older siblings, younger siblings, friends, relatives, and other important people in the child's life can affect whether the child chooses positive or negative options. A jealous struggle with a sister or brother, a

sense of alienation from a stepparent or an embarrassing confrontation with an older child at school may cause the child to use negative options for meeting his or her personal needs.

Sarah's parents couldn't understand why their daughter was suddenly rude and cross at home in the evenings after preschool. After some thought, they realized that Sarah's unexplainable behavior started about the time she began carpooling with Julie, a bossy, older youngster who was belligerent with the other children and even with her own mother. Julie's influence was causing Sarah to choose negative options in her own home.

3. Parental factors. Children are such sensitive creatures that they pick up quickly on times parents are inconsistent or when parents leave some doubt about their love for the child. Even when a parent/child relationship may seem fully intact, children sometimes choose negative options when they think something is amiss between themselves and their parents.

Although Joe prided himself on being a fairly demonstrative father with Todd, his business trips caused him to be away from home excessively. As a result, Todd began to doubt his father's love and blamed himself for Joe's long absences. Todd turned to negative options, such as pinching his baby sister and harming other children's work at preschool.

In working with Joe and Todd, a counselor suggested that young children process information about 90 percent based on their emotional sensitivity and only 10 percent based on their logical reasoning faculties. He helped Joe learn ways to constantly evaluate the quality, consistency, and level of affection and acceptance he was communicating in the parent-child relationship. While Joe could not alter his work-related travel, he could improve his communication with Todd to lessen the psychological stress the absences placed on the child.

OPTION NO. 4—MISINFORMATIONAL

In today's complex world, parents' intentions and expectations for children can become garbled. Even young children can receive mixed messages, or "double binds." This causes them to sense that parents expect them to pursue two seemingly contradictory courses of action or thought.

The parents of Jenny, age four, wanted to develop the child's love of books. They regularly took her to the children's section of the public library and bought her picture books for holidays and birthdays.

Yet, when Jenny brought her parents a book to read, Jenny's mother and dad were consistently too busy to look through the pages with her. When her mother came upon Jenny "reading" a book aloud to herself, she told the child she was being too noisy and silenced her.

Was it any wonder, then, that Jenny eventually began throwing loud and destructive temper tantrums when her mother announced it was time for a library visit? The parents' confusing mixed messages, or lack of clarity in their messages about book reading, caused Jenny to use her negative option of misbehavior.

A counselor could help Jenny's parents untangle and clarify their messages to Jenny about books. All they may need to say is: "I'm glad you want us to read your book, Jenny. It's such a nice book. Mommy has to finish bathing the baby right now, but as soon as he's in bed, we'll curl up on the sofa, just you and me, so we can read."

A related option to misinformation is the option of fear. Especially in their younger years, children seem susceptible to fears that to adults seem irrational. "Various surveys indicate that preschoolers typically have an average of three different fears."[3] Some childhood fears are rational to adults, others are not. For example, both parents and children identify the potential loss of a parent as a major fear, but whereas adults would think that having an operation or a baby in the home would be another significant fear, children see humiliation or embarrassment in front of their peers or flunking a grade as a major fear.

Children who relocate to a new area and have to adjust to a new peer group frequently feel that their self-esteem is in jeopardy as they may not sense the right "fit" with the new group initially. For a while, they may shrink back from interactions with others and almost be ignored by both teachers and peers. Dormant childhood fears typically surface during times of stress or transition for the child.

"In most cases, fears come and go quickly, cause relatively little anxiety, and do not interfere very much with children's lives."[4] In about 5 percent of cases, however, the fear persists and can become an incapacitating dread of some object or event, which constitutes a phobia. A phobia may require professional counseling in order to be corrected.

In helping a young child look for healthy options to deal with his or her fears, we utilize a simple acrostic, called "E.A.R.S. for Fears." Here are its components:

E—*Earnestly listen.* Researchers agree that an earnest and undivided listening ear is the first way to help a child deal with fear. This involves listening and asking open-ended questions that encourage the child to talk further. Parents should avoid drawing conclusions quickly, giving immediate advice or preaching to a child. The fear the child expresses may seem vague, but it nevertheless has been real enough to cause the child great distress.

A—*Accept the child's story.* Be willing to see the situation through the child's eyes. If a young girl feels her clothes make her stand out as "different" from her peers and she senses that they snicker at her for this, don't brush off her fear by saying, "Just don't pay any attention to them. What they say doesn't matter." An adult may minimize the trivial criticisms of an un-enlightened peer group. For the young child, however, such acceptance is the lifeblood of social survival. A parent can learn to see things the way the child sees them. Intellectualizing is wrong at this point.

R—*Reassure.* Parents should reassure children. They do that by trying to help children understand what is going on in their (the children's) world. Children need to know that parents will try to see the future as best they can. As children learn that parents are taking very seriously what is going on and as they see that parents are not angry or confused, but rather are demonstrating confidence, this will become an anchor point for the child. "Being there" for the child, "in season and out," is an important role the parent must play; the counselor can assist in playing this as well.

S—*Suggest.* Suggesting good solution options and supporting the child as he or she tries (and fails) at some options is an important fourth part of how E.A.R.S. can help overcome a child's fears. Support and consistent encouragement by key adults builds a child's sense of worth. In surveying his study, Yamamoto says it clearly: "The basic requirement for everybody, young or old, is to feel that he or she is worth something."[5]

OPTION NO. 5—EMOTIONAL

As we have said earlier, the child's "emotional tank" is kept at a reasonably full level by affection, praise, verbal interaction, or whatever the child needs. If the parent gives reasonable attention to the process, the emotional tank will be kept filled naturally. However, parents should know of opportune times when emotional "tank filling" can occur.

Ross Campbell, in his book, *How to Really Love Your Child*, identifies five periods in which the child is especially open to this process.[6] The first is during times of humor. During a time of mirth and special emotional closeness, the parent can "connect" emotionally with a child simply through sharing eye contact or a special smile or hug. The counselor will notice that such "windows" may occur during the therapy sessions with the family and/or child as family members discuss their home life and shared experiences. A skillful counselor will take advantage of these opportunities.

A second period of receptivity occurs when the child has accomplished something. In such cases, the child is justifiably proud and self-satisfied at the achievement. Appropriate praise and appreciation for a job well done can make significant deposits in the child's emotional tank.

A third receptive period may occur when the child is not physically well. When a child is hurt or becomes ill, his or her emotional "guardrails" are sometimes down. In such times, a special vulnerability occurs in the softer side of parent-child or counselor-to-patient communication. During a time of pain, children may drop their tough or cynical or frivolous exterior and be amazingly touched by adult-like sharing of real feelings and honest concern.

A fourth emotional window occurs during times of personal emotional pain. When a child experiences a significant disappointment, such as losing a close friend or disapproval by a peer group, the parent may find the child especially approachable. The parent may find this a good time to support and genuinely endorse the child's worth. As teen-agers in our practice have

29

said, "It's hard to be cool when you're crying." This applies to children of all ages.

A fifth emotional window occurs around events or holidays or places that have special significance to the child because of past potent experiences. These are highly individual to each particular child. For example, if mealtimes are a particularly rewarding and emotionally rich time for the family, the parent or counselor may find he or she can connect well with the child during such times.

When the child's "emotional tank" is underfilled, the child usually begins to act out by taking negative options that may provoke involvement of others in his or her life. Although this involvement may be negative, the child nevertheless will exercise such negative-option behaviors to make sure others replenish his or her emotional tank. In the child's psychological economy, sometimes negative attention is better than no attention at all.

The child's acting out may take the form of irritating or attention-seeking behavior, intentional failure at tasks, somatic complaints (such as stomachaches or muscle aches and pains), and even self-destructive behavior. Such negative-option behaviors are the child's attempts to fill his or her emotional tank, not only by resisting the process of maturing emotionally but even by outright rebellion against parents and other authority figures.

When the child's emotional tank has been underfilled, corporal punishments such as spankings may not only have little effect on improving behavior but may, in fact, reinforce the negative behavior by producing the desperately needed extra "attention" from the parent. The wise counselor can help the parent discern the difference between the rebellious child who seeks through misbehavior to fill his or her emotional tank and the child who simply is being rebellious toward parental or societal authority. This type of child is discussed in the next example.

OPTION NO. 6—DISOBEDIENT

Disobedience, or the willful rejection of parental or social authority, may at times be the core problem when a child seeks to meet his or her needs. Once parents have explored the physical, psychological, informational, and emotional options as possible explanations for the child's behavior, then they should look at willful disobedience as a possible answer to the problem.

Setting reasonable limits and enforcing these limits by either consequences or spankings (depending on how appropriate spankings are to the child's age and behavior) are crucial elements in helping the child develop responsible behavior. An example of straightforward, willful disobedience at home was shared by a parent at the clinic. Her seven-year-old son had just received an Indian headdress and tomahawk (wooden, thankfully) from his grandmother. His two-year-old sister had received a small doll. Soon, her son was busily "attacking" imaginary foes with his tomahawk while his sister played nearby. The mother told him that the tomahawk was certainly his toy to play with and enjoy, but he must not strike his sister with it. (He had done a war dance around her a couple of times, and Mother could tell what he was tempted to do.)

It had been made clear between them that hitting his little sister with the tomahawk was not permitted (i.e., forbidden fruit, no matter how tempting). The agreement held up for a while. But as Mother worked in the kitchen, she happened to see in the reflection of the bay window a brief interchange around the corner in the den. Her son walked up behind his sister and gave her a brisk whack on the shoulder with his tomahawk. She immediately let out a cry and came running into the kitchen, splurting out her story in broken English. He did not know that Mother had seen the action from the kitchen, and when asked, the boy denied that he had done anything but "show" his sister the tomahawk.

This was not an incident that occurred at the end of the day when the boy was exhausted and fussy. He was not ill, nor was he the victim of favoritism; and he had not been exposed to any psychological trauma. He had simply made a choice to do what he wanted to do in spite of hurting his little sister and disobeying his parent's instruction. He then compounded the infraction by not telling the truth. This was an example of willful disobedience. If the parent does not deal with it firmly (yet with love) the child begins to harbor lowered respect for the parent and can develop confusion about the parent's role as leader in the home.

POSITIVE OPTIONS

Once the parent understands the child's negative options, the parent can work toward setting goals for the child, finding options that are positive. Some ways or goals are:

1. *Trusting and loving relationships* with parents, as opposed to distant, fearful, manipulative, and controlling relationships.

2. *Adaptation* to rules, limits, and expectations on a concrete level. This is done either by parents or in a stable and supportive environment, such as preschool or Sunday school. This type of behavior is the opposite of behavior in which the child believes he or she is exempt from rules and is perennially entitled to do as he or she pleases.

3. *Delayed gratification.* If a child can learn to postpone rewards for short-term goals and instead pursue more desirable long-term goals, this important exercise in self-discipline will widen his or her options to solve problems.

4. *Beginning relationships* with people outside the family. This broadens and deepens the child's repertoire of interpersonal and coping skills.

5. *Sibling relationships and "rivalry."* Learning how to disagree and yet compromise so peace can be maintained is a valuable lesson for young children to learn. Another key lesson is how to forgive and make up within the context of relationships that stay stable.

6. *Keeping the child's "emotional tank" filled* with positive attention. Remember, praise is generally very effective. But avoid putting others down by comparison. Try not to praise indiscriminately or sound phony by showering accolades for everything the child does. Abstain from sarcastic praise, "Well, I can't believe it, you made it to supper on time." Seek to praise the effort more than the sheer success or failure of the outcome.

7. *Appropriate use of "super ego functions."* In other words, helping the child develop a conscience. Learning

the concept of empathy for others and learning the fact that actions have consequences will help the child develop an internal sense of right and wrong. It will also help him or her distinguish between true guilt and false guilt in constructing a conscience that in time, ideally, will be influenced regularly by the Holy Spirit.

8. *A healthy concept of the physical body,* including nutrition and physical abilities. Keeping physically fit and feeling good about one's appearance and level of conditioning helps a child develop responsible and constructive options, rather than destructive ones such as poor nutrition, risk-taking behavior, and physical overactivity.

9. *A healthy concept of mental functions,* including interest in learning, curiosity, and expanding the child's understanding of his or her world. These behaviors would be seen as opposed to negative self-talk, intentional underachievement, deception, or loss of interest in learning.

10. *A healthy concept of sexuality,* appropriate for the children's age. Exploring and resolving sexual gender-identity issues is key in young children's lives and helps them develop a solid sense of selfhood and a belief in personal "wholeness" after experiencing salvation. Most sexual deviations from the normal monogamous heterosexual marriage are relatively easy to trace back to a series of destructive experiences in the past, so it is best to seek for only positive experiences from an early age.

11. *Strong parental input* to counteract various negative outside influences, such as television. The amount of time television takes away—time that families otherwise could be using to interact—is staggering. Parents also need to help children understand the impact that advertising has on them. Children need to understand that a product isn't necessarily desirable just because a movie star or an amusing animal helps promote it.

For example, the value of a product or the desirability of a lifestyle being depicted through the media can be discussed with the child by the parent spontaneously as the opportunity presents itself. Questions during a television commercial can be raised, like: "I wonder why that car company makes it look like so much fun to own one of its cars? Do you think some people might see this commercial and want to buy one of those cars, even if they really didn't have enough money to afford it?" Children can readily develop the habit of thinking through the overt messages they are receiving from the media, and can see it as an enjoyable game to determine what they're really saying to the viewers in the commercials.

CHAPTER FOUR

WAYS FOR CHANGE WITH
THE YOUNG CHILD

PARENTS NEED LOOK NO FARTHER than the Scriptures to find a guideline for producing positive change in the young child. Proverbs 22:6 speaks of this when it admonishes, "Train up a child in the way he should go: and when he is old, he will not depart from it" (KJV).

That successful training of which the Bible speaks occurs when parents take significant actions to change the child's negative options into positive ones. Using effective ways for change to shape the child's personality also is the fundamental building block to all counseling.

Six categories exist for implementing change in the young child. The first of these, relationships, is so significant it occupies the remainder of this chapter. The other five—goals, expectations, responsibilities, limits and consequences, and a spiritual life—are discussed in chapter 5.

PARENT-TO-PARENT RELATIONSHIPS

Three major relationships affect the young child. These are: (1) parent-to-parent, (2) child-to-mother, and (3) child-to-father relationships.

The first of these, parent-to-parent relationships, has to do with the quality of the marriage relationship in the home. Since the child directly observes these key people in his or her life, the quality of this relationship substantially affects the child's concept of trust in the possibility of stability.

Especially in terms of relationships, children model much of what they see. Much of this is unconscious; yet, the counselor should help the parents understand that children are continually assessing, internalizing, and often eventually reproducing both the positive and negative aspects of the key relationships in which their parents are involved.

"Many people behave toward their children in the same manner as their parents did toward them," says Martin Goldberg of the division of family study in the University of Pennsylvania's School of Medicine. He notes that if a son observes his father frequently contradicting his mother's decisions, for example, the son later may act in the same manner when he marries.[1]

A most devastating negative aspect of the parent-to-parent relationship, which can have a profound adverse effect on the young child, is parental sabotage. This occurs when one spouse undermines the authority of the other.

Roughly four types of parental sabotage exist. They are active, passive, internal, and indirect. *Active sabotage* occurs when one spouse takes actions directly interfering with the attempted parental actions of the other. For example, this could occur if the mother schedules gymnastics lessons for a child and the father refuses to pay for the lessons or refuses to drive the children to the lessons.

Passive parental sabotage involves using indecisiveness, forgetfulness, procrastination, or overscheduling to sabotage a decision or course of action. For example, if the parents have agreed on certain chores for the family to perform, the mother could continually "forget" which chores were assigned to the children, thereby allowing the children to evade their responsibilities without absolutely refusing to do so.

Internal sabotage occurs when one parent is too ill, too depressed, too confused, or too anxious to follow through on plans or agreements entered into with the other spouse. An example is the mother who constantly has a headache, a backache, a stomachache, or some type of malady that keeps her from helping her children with their homework even though the parents (and the teacher) have agreed that is necessary to help bring up grades.

This kind of sabotage is especially hard to deal with because it often either mimics or actually capitalizes on real physical or emotional problems. Unfortunately, the other spouse's sympathy for the saboteur who continually uses internal sabotage, in time, will run out. Then some major conflict may occur in the home.

Indirect sabotage occurs when one parent uses a third party to help undermine the authority of the other parent. Using in-laws or grandparents is a classic technique in indirect sabotage. In divorce situations, former spouses commonly use the children to help sabotage the plans of the other parent.

Parental sabotage is damaging because it makes life difficult for the spouses involved and also confuses the child about exactly what is expected of him or her. Even worse, it creates a legacy of contradiction, exclusion, and imposition which can be passed on from generation to generation.

Contraindication (one parent siding differently from the other), exclusion (one parent excluding the other from the decision-making process), or imposition (one parent allowing his or her own beliefs or the beliefs of others to dominate family decisions) constitute the barbs of parental sabotage.

In helping a couple avoid parental sabotage, the counselor should involve as many family members as possible during treatment. This especially should occur in the evaluation process. At that point, particular areas of need in either spouse can be focused on. The discovery of these may lead to individual counseling.

If grandparents or stepparents are contributing to the parental sabotage, the therapist should include them if possible. The counselor should encourage the family members to recognize what component each plays. This should occur without shifting blame or dumping the entire blame for the problem onto any one spouse or family member.

Helping families in which much parental sabotage has existed may be a long and difficult struggle. It requires reestablishing basic trust, plus new means of communicating and decision-making. But the outcome of this process in developing a healthy personality in the child makes all the effort worthwhile.

MOTHER-TO-CHILD RELATIONSHIPS

The mother-child relationship greatly affects the child's ability to appropriately meet his or her emotional needs throughout life. Mothers should be nurturing but not overbearing.

Mothers must at times sacrifice their own emotional needs in the short run in order to meet the child's current needs. True fairness actually does not exist in the mother-child bond. At least in the early childhood years, this relationship is a one-way street in which the mother meets the child's basic personality (narcissistic) needs but can expect the child not to meet the mother's needs in return.

The mother must teach by example and patience. She often will find herself handling difficult and confusing situations by patiently asking questions and by allowing her children to express their true feelings, not just by giving answers. She consistently must demonstrate she can remain emotionally stable and sensitive while also carrying out a consistent and effective plan of action in a multitude of situations.

The effective mother must avoid becoming any of the following four mothering types:

1. The "Smothering" Mother: This smother-mother attempts to meet all her child's needs. In fact, many times, she actually seeks to meet her own emotional needs through feeding off the child's needs. The smother-mother rarely lets the child learn from his or her own mistakes and always seeks to shield the child from such situations as discomfort, setbacks, and shame.

She quickly runs to school when the child repeatedly forgets to take his lunch. She instantly intercedes with teachers when the child is reprimanded in class or makes a bad grade, even though the child may deserve the reprimand and may make the bad grade due to poor study habits.

Although well meaning, the smother-mother unfortunately often thwarts the child's healthy emotional development when she filters out many independence-producing experiences the child needs to encounter.

2. The "Vampire" Mother: This mother seeks to find virtually all her personal fulfillment in living through her offspring's childhood. This mother often regrets missing out on certain emotional experiences in her upbringing. She relives her own childhood through her child.

A classic example of this type is the mother who pushes her child to be a cheerleader or high-school beauty queen because the mother herself feels she wasn't pretty or popular during her own growing-up days. Children with such mothers often feel guilty and insecure about growing up. They fear that if they mature, their mother will not be able to handle the natural separation that comes when a child leaves the nest of home.

3. The "Overwhelmed" Mother: This mother feels she can't handle situations, and so she often doesn't handle them well. She essentially disconnects from the children emotionally or even physically; hence, she finds a myriad of interests outside the home.

Children with this type of mother begin to fear it is their own fault that the mother isn't involved with them. Therefore, the children feel unloved at some level. The myriad activities, lessons, and special treats such a mother may provide for the children do not compensate for their feeling that she is unwilling to be available emotionally to them.

Under such an influence, children often develop a life-long sense of inner emptiness. They will be unable to feel secure in the love of other persons because they lack the vigorous emotional bond with their own mothers. In a world filled with creative activities, where children are lavished with material things and blessed with educational opportunities, these children can become the invisible, psychologically "walking-wounded" victims of the overwhelmed, busy, and emotionally absent mother.

4. The "Zoo-keeper" Mother: This mother often is hassled and frustrated by the ordinary emotional and physical demands of her child or children. She often has several children, and the constant emotional drain of the experience begins to psychologically wear her down.

This mother tends to use "put downs" and "voice ups" to seek to corral her children and to manipulate their behavior. For example, if a child has spilled something once too often, the zoo-keeper mother might say, "What's the matter with you? Are you trying out for the role of clumsiest child in the world?" Such a statement may make the child more conscious of clumsy behavior in the future, but the indelible scar it inflicts upon the child's self-concept is hardly worth it.

In her use of "voice ups," the mother yells or screams in an effort to control the child's behavior. Seeing herself as having less and less control over a difficult-to-manage child, she may use intimidating, loud words to nullify the child's behavior.

The myth that children respond more readily to louder voice commands is just that—a myth. In fact, some recent scientific studies have revealed that when parents communicate in a yelling or screaming mode, children actually hear less of what the parents say.[2]

Other Sunday school teachers were always amazed that Lavonne, an extremely soft-spoken woman, kept her pupils at rapt attention. Actually, lowering her voice was part of Lavonne's technique. She found that as the pupils strained to hear some of her words, they quietened down in the process.

Just as a person will duck to avoid a lightning bolt, the child may change his or her immediate course of behavior after a sharply yelled command; but the yelled command imparts no lasting character change.

A good rule of thumb is this: When the mother finds herself raising her voice at the child to communicate commands and expectations, she probably needs to reassess how effective her relationship is with the child at that moment. There is truth in the saying, "A screaming sailor reflects a sinking ship."

FATHER-TO-CHILD RELATIONSHIPS

The father-to-child relationship will help the child develop important ways for positive change as the child matures. The father has at least four key functions within the home:

Father Function No. 1—Provider. The father must provide financial support, a secure living situation, and a sense of general stability. These contributions are crucial to the young child's belief that the world is a trustworthy place. The Scripture says a father who will not provide for his own family is "worse than an infidel" (1 Tim. 5:8 KJV).

The necessity of this function may require a father to set aside his natural entrepreneurial instincts and change his lifestyle in order to provide a cocoon of security for the child. Uncertainty and business risks may bring exhilaration to the father, but it can be unsettling and frightening to children growing up in the home.

The father also is responsible to see that the child experiences those things that are normal in the birth-to-age-six time frame, such as opportunities to understand and inquire about the mysteries of life. Counselors need to help fathers see that failing to spend time with their children in this age bracket amounts to abdicating their parental responsibility to provide for their children. Fathers may supply material blessings aplenty, but that does not fulfill the biblical mandate to fully provide for their children.

One father, feeling guilty because a new job was requiring great chunks of his time, bought his son an expensive but useless robot the first Christmas after his job transfer. Later, the father realized he had overindulged the son in an effort to compensate for the time he had been unable to give. Meanwhile, the son began to act out through temper tantrums and other defiant misbehaviors. Instead of buying more material gifts for his son, the dad altered his work schedule to spend more time with his son, and the boy's mood improved.

According to Wilson Grant, "Children spell love T-I-M-E. . . . But the amount of time that we spend with our children is not the only issue. The quality of that time also is important."[3]

Unfortunately, fathers sometimes think quality time means dreaming up unusual or rather outlandish activities which mesmerize the child and make an indelible impression. In order to capture the child's attention, some fathers plan extravagant and expensive outings to amusement parks, recreational facilities, or other places. Yet that isn't necessary. A parent can spend quality time with the child simply by paying attention to the child and by strategically listening to the child's comments when parent and child are together. While listening to a "Focus on the Family" broadcast, we once heard the statement, "Wherever you are, be *all* there." We like to use this in helping fathers understand the best way to have quality time with their children.

Being available to the child when key experiences occur is crucial. As Gordon MacDonald says, "Ineffective fathers usually miss the value of a child's bedtime because they are caught up with 'significant' matters like 'Monday Night Football,' endless meetings outside the home, and snoozes on the couch."[4]

The present-day emphasis on fathers sharing more of the parental role with the wife is, hopefully, a part of the reason that fathers may be spending more time with their children. Studies indicate the average father spent 137 minutes per week in child care in 1976, and 173 minutes in similar child care in 1982. This represents a significant increase.[5]

Michael Lamb of the University of Utah says, "Children with highly-involved fathers are characterized by increased cognitive competence, increased empathy, less sex-stereotyped beliefs and a greater sense of their own potency rather than seeing themselves as at the mercy of uncontrollable external forces."[6] As counselors, a saying we like to use with the fathers whom we counsel is, "If *you* aren't influencing your child, someone else is."

Father Function No. 2—Protector. The father must protect the child from dangers and from negative influences outside the home, inside the home, and even inside the child. The father must be aware of the neighborhood in which his child is growing up; he must know who lives in that neighborhood and what is its level of security. Neglecting the potential dangers to the child can result in unnecessary tragedies.

Dangers also exist inside the home. The father, along with

the mother, must be sure the home is a safe place in which to grow up. They must be sure strangers, including baby-sitters and individuals visiting the home, in no way jeopardize the young child.

To be sure, the father shares all these functions with his wife, but an effective father does not shirk his overall responsibility to ensure that the child is not harassed or intimidated by other siblings in their home. For example, intimidation can occur from siblings through taunting, ridicule, or pointing out a physical flaw in the child. The parents must detect and seek to eliminate this.

The father also must protect the child from his or her own impulses. Young children often have destructive impulses; at best, they show behavior that is immature and reflects poor judgment. As the child grows, these behaviors will diminish if the child is properly parented. But in the early years, the father, along with the mother, must help not only protect the child from the consequences of these actions, but must also train the child to reduce impulsive actions and to work within limits set by authority figures.

A father also protects his children when he does not permit a child to vent his or her anger destructively against a sibling. Father prevents the sibling-victim from being injured or emotionally intimidated and also protects the sibling-perpetrator from creating the seedbed for a long-standing poor relationship.

A father, with his wife, also must protect his children from outside forces, such as harmful television and radio programs, movies, harmful teachings at school and even Sunday school, and the conduct of visiting children in the home.

Jack began to observe that his son Jason was rude and defiant at home only after a certain neighbor friend spent the night with Jason. Regular as clockwork, Jason would begin talking back haughtily to his parents whenever the neighbor child stayed in Jason's home for any length of time. The father also noticed the neighbor was more out of control than were any of Jason's other friends. Jack discreetly worked to limit the chances the two boys had to be together for long periods. When the boys did visit, Jack kept on guard to set limits immediately whenever behavior approached an unacceptable level.

Naturally, the father must seek a balance in this. No father should be an overbearing "super-censor" who attempts to purify his child's world totally. However, in most cases, fathers appear to be too passive or disinterested in the fact that their family's spiritual or psychological values often are assaulted.

Father Function No. 3—Spiritual Leader. The father's role as spiritual leader in the home is not a matter for self-pride or arrogance, but rather has to do with responsibility for obedience to God's scriptural command to teach his ways to the children.

> And these words, which I am commanding you today, shall be on your heart; and you shall teach them diligently to your sons and shall talk of them when you sit in your house and when you walk by the way and when you lie down and when you rise up. (Deut. 6:6, 7)

This role will be addressed more fully in the section titled, "The Spiritual Training of the Child" at the end of chapter 5. The father's responsibility for the spiritual development of his children cannot be abdicated to his spouse, to the church, or to any outside sources. Key factors in communicating concepts of God to the child include the following:

a. Accept the images of God that the child has. A child may understand God in a vague fashion, but such an understanding is perfectly acceptable in a young child. Young children may see God as an old fellow who floats on the clouds. However, in time, they will understand the majesty and abstract issues of grace, sanctification, and eternal fellowship.

b. Admit that no parent fully understands about God or the Scriptures. Children are wise enough to see through pat answers or easy explanations to tough questions. The father may not be able to give readily understandable reasons why a pet died or why a disaster occurred. But dads can share the fact that they, too, struggle with certain perplexing questions about God.

c. Cast God in the light of love and continual care. One of a child's primary fears is that he or she will be abandoned, punished without cause, or humiliated. Casting God in the light of a caring and consistently available father is crucial to the child's early concept of God.

d. Demonstrate your values in action. Much of God's "reputation" in the child's mind comes from the degree of consistency, dependability, and loving acceptance the parents demonstrate. The maxim that children believe 90 percent of what parents do and 10 percent of what parents say may be accurate not only for the child's image of the parent but also for the child's early concept of God.

e. Let children see God in the context of a family relationship. They must see the practice of faith occurring in the context of mutually rewarding and fulfilling relationships between adults. A child can more easily sense the concept of God as a father and the church as a living organism when that child sees Dad having close friendships in the church, when Bible studies occur in the home, and when Christian friends are seen to help one another through tough times. The father's role as spiritual leader certainly involves making God's existence seem real, God's influence seem constant, and God's presence seem reassuring.

Father Function No. 4—Pacesetter. The father must lead by example. He must set the pace for spiritual growth, emotional health, honesty, and consistency in the home. Children will follow a model. If given the opportunity, a child will follow someone's lead in virtually every situation. If the father is not providing that leadership, the child will find the leader somewhere else.

This does not minimize the mother's impact as part of the family leadership team. However, in our clinical observations, we have seen that the child likely will gather a large amount of his or her values from sources outside the home if the father capitulates as the home's pacesetter.

Parents of teen-agers often say, "We just don't know where they (the teens) got that idea." Frequently, however, unhealthy beliefs and concepts work their way into the home because the father has abdicated his role as a true pacesetter for the children to model. Divergent ideals and rebellious lifestyle patterns grow in the fertile soil of a leaderless home. A father should not assume he has to be perfect in order to model for his child. Neither should the father assume that the role of model will always be enjoyable—but it is crucial.

One writer has suggested some principles of spiritual leadership that apply to fathers:

a. A father should be thankful to God and demonstrate commitment to God in his home. A father who continually pushes his family toward achievement and who does not stop to enjoy what family members have accomplished or to appreciate them as individuals soon will discourage his family. Family members feel they can never do enough to please Dad, so why make the effort?

b. A father should have a spirit of genuine humility. Dad must be willing to admit he's wrong, to accept a mistake as being his own, and not shift blame to others or attempt to rationalize his shortfalls. His wife and children will appreciate his honesty and will take real pride in his transparency rather than assuming their husband and father is prideful or that he attempts to be a "Superman."

c. A father should learn to be in control of his emotions and his tongue. Even though Dad should be transparent with his emotions and true beliefs, he should not explode with harsh words, thoughtless statements, or destructive actions. Rebukes or harsh criticisms cutting to the very soul of a child can be like a cancer, doing deadly damage years later to the child's adult self-image.

d. A father should be kind and show good manners. Some people believe the traits of simple courtesy and gentlemanly deference to others are becoming extinct in the American male. A good dad treats his wife with great respect. He remembers special events and is attentive.

e. A father should accept each person in the family as he or she really is. He must not compare members of his family with other persons of greater ability or achievement. He should not use put downs or "you'll never" statements to try to force his children into a mold they were never meant to fit. A father must assure his children that each was greatly wanted and that each is a special provision to him from the Lord.

f. A father needs to earn the right to be heard. Although God assigns to the father the role of spiritual head of his home, respect must be earned. Dad does not demand respect. He should earn privileges by developing relationships within his family in such a way as to spawn a sense of appreciation and reverent respect for Dad's lifestyle, his love for the family, and his commitment to Christ.[7]

Men who are willing to demonstrate these qualities are rare. Yet the fathers in our society who do so will set a pace of knowing God and living by his Word that constitutes hope for future generations. Alexander Solzhenitsyn, the Soviet dissident, wrote:

> If I were called upon to identify the principal trait of the entire twentieth century, hereto I would be unable to find anything more precise and pithy than to repeat once again: Men have forgotten God.

A nation whose fathers know the Lord will be a nation whose sons and daughters know the Lord.

It is said that a mother's love is more of a nurturing love while the father's is more of an enabling love. Of course, each can contain elements of the other. But both types of love must be in abundant supply in the home if the parents wish to establish the child's trust and autonomy and subsequently to establish a healthy self-identity.

CHAPTER FIVE

MORE WAYS FOR CHANGE WITH THE YOUNG CHILD

KIMBERLY HAD TROUBLE PARENTING TIM, a high-energy child who could not seem to learn to play by himself and who demanded constant social interaction. She struggled to adjust to this fireball because she expected her child to be placid and easy-going, as she was when growing up. Kimberly's troubles eased when she finally accepted the fact that Tim was not her personality clone.

As one of her goals for Tim, Kimberly determined she would recognize innate differences between her personality and her child's temperamental disposition. When she stopped trying to make Tim fit her model of normal, she was able to reach a happy meeting point in her relationship with the youngster. She then began to make better parenting decisions.

GOALS

After focusing on the key relationships within the home, as discussed in chapter 4, the parents should focus on the proper use of goals in the change process.

Goals, such as the one Kimberly set with Tim, are for equipping the child. They should be clear, reinforceable, and should contribute to the child's greater self-confidence and self-esteem. Goals can help deepen the quality of relationships as they give the child an opportunity to work with another person in solving problems. Goals for certain behaviors also can improve a child's development of habit patterns promoting health and safety. Also, goals can provide good avenues for improving self-discipline and impulse controls.

Possibly with the help of a counselor, parents should talk over goals openly and extensively before sharing them with the child. Sometimes parents can get help from other couples who have successfully parented children through the age group of their child. Other couples can share the goals that they used successfully and can share how they reinforced those goals. A wise counselor can take advantage of other parental resources in the church or community to support parents who struggle with establishing and implementing goals in the family unit.

A key principle to remember is that *goals exist to serve the child.* The child does not exist to serve goals. In helping parents set reasonable goals for their children, the counselor can suggest some guidelines:

1. Learn to distinguish between the child's behavior that is temperamentally induced (constitutional) and that which is learned. For example, if a child knocks over the parent's best lamp because he is by temperament a high-energy child, that is a different behavior than if he deliberately knocks over the lamp.

The counselor must assist the parents in understanding the child's natural temperament and realize that temperament probably cannot be fundamentally changed, even though it can be channeled in appropriate ways. One simply cannot hope to change a child who is by nature active and outgoing into one who is shy and introverted.

49

2. Learn to deal with behavior situations from a position of anticipation rather than reaction. Parents can learn to use distractions and situational alterations to defuse situations rather than having to confront the child.

For example, to avoid a confrontation with a highly energetic child about bedtime, the parent can help the child distinguish between "bedtime" and "go-to-sleep" time. Parents could still insist that the child go to bed at a certain hour, but they would give him or her time to "wind down," quietly reading or engaging in some quiet activity in bed until sleep comes.

3. Learn to set firm consequences when the child obviously engages in deliberate disobedience or destructiveness. Helping the parents become experts at understanding their own child's nature and distinguishing between tantrums and temperament is important. This can go a long way toward helping parents develop the fortitude to follow through on limits and consequences for oppositional behavior.

EXPECTATIONS

The old adage, "I love the sinner but hate the sin," was never more appropriate than when studying expectations. The child must always feel totally accepted—that Mom and Dad love him or her unconditionally, whether they approve of the child's actions or not.

In setting expectations, parents must communicate *acceptance* differently than they do *approval*. This is crucial to the child's self-worth. Expectations are standards upon which the parent will base his or her approval of the child's behavior. The child must never feel he or she is in danger of losing love or "belongingness" because of divergent or inappropriate behavior.

Parents must communicate their expectations to the child concerning such matters as fighting with peers, knowing right from wrong, and being responsible to properly maintain personal property. However, parents must communicate a sense that no transgression or shortcoming can sever the lines of acceptance and love that exist between parent and child. Communicating this is essential for a child's development of a healthy personality.

Unfortunately, some adults struggle throughout their entire lives for more and more approval. They hope one day to gain the acceptance that they never felt in their homes as children. Some people never find it.

RESPONSIBILITIES

Progressively giving a child increasing amounts of responsibility is like properly firing a porcelain vase. If, on the other hand, the vase is not fired long enough or hotly enough, it may be weak although it appears well-formed. Such would be the case of a child not given freedom to develop a strong sense of responsibility for actions and choices as he or she grows.

In introducing this way for change, the counselor will point out that though responsibilities are somewhat like expectations, they have more to do with the child's increasing level of control over his or her own world. With increasing responsibilities should come increasing privileges and greater freedom. Children begin at birth with essentially no responsibilities. Responsibilities should progress slowly until the late teen-age years, when a child has a great deal of responsibility for monitoring his or her own lifestyle.

The process of parenting is the process of slowly, progressively letting go of our children, like one finger at a time releasing a dove from our hands to fly away.

The use of chores or household tasks is a highly valuable and well-proven way to help children develop responsibility and a sense of personal confidence. A forty-year study by George E. Vaillant, a psychiatrist from Dartmouth College, showed an amazingly strong correlation between happy young adult men and the fact that as boys they had worked at various chores, responsibilities, and part-time jobs outside the home. These men reported they had close relationships and a sense of personal fulfillment as adults. Many of them were from poor or broken homes. Yet, being disadvantaged did not prove to be a limiting factor in their ultimate success. Rather, their success seemed to stem from whether they as youngsters learned responsibilities from working hard and having assigned duties.[1]

The following Eight-A Approach to responsibilities may help the family with young children:

1. *Address the real purpose for chores.* The real objective in teaching children is not necessarily to make them experts at taking out the trash or masterful dishwashers. The purpose is to help children understand what cooperative work is and to aid them in feeling they are worthwhile members of their small society—the family—and later, their community. In describing this phenomenon, Vaillant in his forty-year study said, "Boys who worked in the home or community gained competence and came to feel they were worthwhile members of society. And because they felt good about themselves, others felt good about them."[2]

2. *Age is a factor.* Beginning chores at very young ages is a good idea as long as the task is appropriate. Children naturally want to cooperate with their parents and "join in" to model parents' behavior. A father hammering a board in the garage may turn to see that his son has been observing him and now, trying to be "just like Dad," is nailing some ragged piece of wood with a makeshift hammer of his own. Parents should make chores and responsibilities fun as much as possible.

3. *Assign simple and repetitive tasks.* Children learn primarily by simple repetition. A task that is consistent and repetitive in its nature often is easier to learn than is one requiring judgment and change each time it's performed. For example, assigning a young child the responsibility of keeping the back patio neat may be more difficult for the child to do properly than will the concrete assignment of lining the bicycles along one wall and making sure all balls and bats are in a box by the back door. Youngsters can better develop more abstract responsibilities that pertain to quality and motivation in the later grade-school and early adolescent years than in early childhood.

4. *Allow the job to stand.* Parents who pick up what the children missed, correct their mistakes and generally redo the job may send unintentional messages to the child. One message is that his or her contribution or performance is not

acceptable. The second message is that adequate completion of the job is not all that important because Mom or Dad
will come along and make it right anyway. An eleven-year-
old once described what a mother should do to be good at
child-rearing: "You only need to know three things about
kids. Don't hit them too much, don't yell at them too much
and don't do too much for them."[3]

5. *Abstain from bribery.* Don't get into the habit of paying a child for routine duties. It only develops the sense of
entitlement. Money paid for allowances or for specific jobs
above and beyond normal responsibilities is acceptable
and should be encouraged. A child who is paid to brush his
teeth may assume that he also should be paid to finish
his homework or to avoid punching his little sister in the
nose. Parents should teach children the spirit of cooperation and community effort without rendering them too
mercenary in their motives.

6. *Appreciate whenever possible.* Although negative reinforcement may help when direct misconduct or disrespect
or dishonesty is involved, positive reinforcement should be
used as much as possible. Appreciation works especially
well when children show commitment to a task or good
work habits. A pat on the back, a smile at the appropriate
time, and a word of thanks from a pleased parent go a long
way to instill in a child a sense of joint accomplishment and
self-satisfaction.

7. *Avoid overdoing it.* Even though responsibilities and
chores are important, childhood needs to be a time of joy
and relative carefreeness. The child should not be bur-
dened with so many requirements and duties that he or she
begins to lose the joys of childhood. At best, childhood is a
short period of time, packed with myriad events that are
potent for forming lasting patterns in the character.

Some parents with several children—among them a
highly responsible firstborn child—let that firstborn function as a third parent. A twelve-year-old with employed
parents may look like the epitome of a mature young person as she cares for her younger siblings after school and on
weekends. However, she may feel a sense of deep regret

and disappointment that she is missing out on some of her "rights" to have a childhood of her own. Counselors who work with high-achieving families will want to be aware of this potential phenomenon.

8. *Accessibility to outside jobs and responsibilities is encouraged.* A child who accepts jobs outside the home in his or her late grade-school or early teen-age years learns many valuable lessons. The young boy who mows yards or the young girl who baby-sits learns important lessons about employer-employee relationships and about adjusting to various people's needs and personalities. These, of course, have to do with the older child.

LIMITS AND CONSEQUENCES

Applying limits and consequences is crucially important because of its role in training the child. However, parents should avoid using limits and consequences in ways that can become abusive. The counselor can suggest three basic types of interventions in this subject area:

1. *Situational interventions* (time-outs). Time-outs can deescalate or defuse a situation when direct negative reinforcement, such as a spanking, seems to be ineffective in correcting a situation and/or conveying a principle. Timeouts especially help, for example, in the case of a sibling fight when no clear perpetrator exists. Some intervention is needed. If both children are squabbling over a raft in the wading pool, the parent avoids taking sides but asks both of them to leave the water for a ten-minute time-out.

2. *Consequential interventions* (loss or curtailment of privileges). For children four through six, realizing that a disobedient or irresponsible act carries certain natural consequences can be a valuable lesson. For example, the boy who fails to retrieve his baseball equipment from the yard even after his parents have reminded him may learn a valuable lesson when his glove and cap are soaked by a rainstorm or by the early-morning sprinkler system. Parents should take care that consequences do not

genuinely harm the child. However, consequences have a way of teaching lessons that direct parental intervention sometimes does not.

3. *Corporal interventions* (spankings). The hand spank is especially useful in times of direct disobedience, deception, or disrespect, when an issue of the will is involved. Naturally, a parent should be in control of his or her emotions when the spanking occurs. Also, children should understand in advance that a spanking is the consequence for this type of misbehavior. Children inherently know the difference between an appropriate spanking from a concerned and loving parent, and an angry outburst or physical violence.

Although these limits and consequences can work with any type of child, they may be crucial in working with an "oppositional," or strong-willed, child. Such a child is characterized by frequent temper tantrums, assaultiveness (usually against mother or a younger sibling, rarely against father), excessive demands for attention, defiance (often accompanied by threats and physical striking out), overactive behavior, a quick anger, and stubbornness.

As for "overactive" behavior, the oppositional child cannot classically be diagnosed as having an attention deficit disorder. He or she appears set on staging small battles of defiance and self-will wherever the opportunity presents itself.

With reference to anger, this child's moods often fluctuate between being satisfied and being enraged at others. Parents with an oppositional child sometimes say the child is either an angel or a demon—an angel when he gets his way, and a demon when he doesn't.

As for stubbornness, the oppositional child persists in getting his or her own way even when the negative consequences of this persistence outweigh any possible gains. The oppositional child seeks to win a confrontation even at the cost of losing something more desirable. For example, the oppositional child may refuse to buckle into a car seat, even though he or she knows this will cause the parents to cancel the trip to the ice cream store.

THE SPIRITUAL TRAINING OF THE CHILD

Both parents are responsible to God to properly expose their children to spiritual training. The father and the mother should help ground the child in a firm understanding of God's character and also in the relationship God wants to have with his children. This also will help the child understand the relationship God wants to have with his people in general, the church.

In essence, the spiritual training of a child between birth and age six revolves around two central commandments in Scripture:

> "'You shall love the Lord your God with all your heart, and with all your soul, and with all your mind.' This is the great and foremost commandment. The second is like it, 'You shall love your neighbor as yourself.'" (Matt. 22:37–39)

The following seven items constitute a brief spiritual thermometer. With it, the counselor can determine if parents are addressing key elements in the young child's early spiritual training.

Reflection

The child should learn the love of God through the parents' love, patience, and tenderness. The child also should see God's uprightness and decency in parents' character qualities.

Position

The child needs to learn that God never changes and that he indeed loves the child very much. In the fifth and sixth year of life, the child becomes acutely aware of the concept of disobedience and of breaking rules. At this point, the child easily can be taught the concept of sin as our disobedience to God. The child can realize the fact that Jesus died and took away our sins so we would not have to be punished for them. The five- or six-year-old begins to understand that everyone has done wrong deeds that deserve punishment, but also that God loves us and offers us forgiveness through Jesus Christ.

Children this age will have an easier time understanding the substitutionary death of Jesus Christ if it is presented in terms they can understand—such as a story. For example, a father learned that his son was guilty of breaking many laws in the land. He had broken so many laws that it was determined that the only way he could be punished was for him to die. Once the father learned that his son was to die, he was very sad. Because of his great love for his son, he offered that his own life be taken in order that his son might live. As children begin to understand the fact that Jesus died for them, it does much to secure in their own minds their position of importance and their value to God.

Inclusion

The child should be learning to talk about the Lord and to include him in daily activities, plans, and thoughts. This helps bring God down to the day-to-day coming and going of the child's life. The child should learn to turn to Jesus for help when frightened, lonely, or anxious. Such experiences will help the child understand the meaning of having faith in God and trusting him during different situations.

This also is an important way to begin to teach the child the joy and excitement of the Christian life. The child can see that the Christian life is not a ritualistic or stagnant religion, but an abundant and practical relationship with the Creator of the universe. A child can learn that knowing and relating to the Creator is the most natural thing in the world.

Nutrition

The child needs to feed regularly on the Word of God through reading Bible stories (or having them read), attending Sunday school, memorizing verses, and other practices. This should not be overbearing or burdensome for the child. The parents should make sure that exposure to the Scripture is as creative and as fun as possible. In assisting the family with young children, the counselor should reinforce this point.

Children bored with dry, didactic concepts they cannot process soon begin to assume that participating in the Christian life is more burdensome than it is freeing. Christian bookstores overflow with creative and sparkling new ideas to make the Scriptures interesting and accessible to young minds.

Also, children need to learn to pray. This helps them digest and put into perspective the material they learn from the Scriptures.

Connection

Children in the five- and six-year-old age bracket can ridicule and ostracize greatly. We help the child by teaching him or her about God's interest in our *connecting* with, loving, and supporting others. The ability to empathize and identify with others is a crucial way-point in children's developing spirituality. Learning not to criticize others, not to make fun of the faults of others, and not to gossip about others are crucial teaching opportunities for the young child.

Parents can say things to their child like, "How do you think Dan felt when his classmates teased him about his limp?" By trying to put themselves in others' shoes, children can develop a true sense of compassion that will mark the rest of their lives.

Submission

Children should learn to share themselves in an attitude of servanthood to others. This means learning to share, learning not to be selfish, and learning not always to demand their own way. Children who receive encouragement and support at home will have a strong self-image. They can learn subjection without becoming passive or a "doormat."

Five-year-old Shelley accompanied her parents as their Sunday school class participated in a "paint-up, fix-up" project for some elderly people's homes. Shelley "helped" by holding the ladder steady for her dad while he climbed. The event took some of the family's precious weekend time, but the lesson it taught Shelley about sharing with others was worth more to her future than any weekend amusement park outing could be.

The ability to selectively set aside one's own interests to serve another human being is a spiritual trait all too often overlooked in the modern church. The foundations of this spiritual trait often are laid in the early years of life.

Perfection

Children should learn to accept themselves in light of how God sees them and who God says they are. They can learn that God will perpetually move them toward increasing Christlikeness and perfection. Even in their early formative years, children can learn a healthy understanding of the frailty of mankind and of God's continual love, acceptance, and forgiveness.

In all of these areas, parents will want to reflect realistically on how the child has progressed in becoming more Christlike. They will not manipulate the child with too-flowery praise or subtle "you-didn't-quite-measure-up" criticisms. Both approaches tend to stifle the child's spiritual development and quell the urge to press forward in pursuing Christlikeness. Finally, the counselor should encourage parents to identify with the child and let him or her see that they experience both success and failure in their pursuit of maturity in Christ.

CHAPTER SIX

SPECIFIC PROBLEMS AND DISORDERS OF THE YOUNG CHILD

ANN, A YOUNG WOMAN JUST OUT OF COLLEGE, became employed at her first job. It was in a museum development office. Her new coworkers thought Ann attractive and intelligent, but they also perceived her as a bit arrogant and unfriendly. This perception became a handicap that kept Ann from making valuable associations at work in those first crucial days on the job.

However, Ann's demeanor was not due to arrogance, but to shyness, a trait Ann had exhibited from childhood. Like many other traits, shyness does not represent a clinical diagnosis or specific emotional illness. Instead, it is merely a problem associated with the training and rearing of the young child. In Ann's case, if a counselor or parent had made a healthy intervention regarding her shyness during her childhood, it might have prevented her work-related difficulties later.

In this chapter, we will take a further look at shyness and other common childhood disorders.

THE SHY CHILD

Shy children frequently are described as timid, easily frightened, distrustful, bashful, modest, reserved, and hesitant to commit themselves to activities or relationships. They become anxious when they think about social failure or criticism, and they withdraw from social situations. Lack of self-confidence, fear of new situations, and fear of being hurt are typical in shy, withdrawn children.

Periods of normal shyness occur at about five or six months of age and again at age two. But even outside these ages, the incidence of shyness is very high. Researchers say approximately 40 percent of all children at one time or another are described as shy.[1] The child who is consistently shy risks developing problems when he or she tries to initiate and maintain interpersonal relationships and resolve conflicts.

Several reasons exist for the symptoms of shyness:

1. Avoidance. The avoidant child is one who exhibits excessive shrinking from contact with unfamiliar people to a degree that it interferes with social functioning in peer relationships. *The Diagnostic and Statistics Manual–III–Revised* (DSM-III–R) says these children demonstrate a desire for close contact only with people who are familiar to them, especially close family members. These children must be carefully supported and reinforced in their growing contacts with the world outside the family. Their progress will be slow because they avoid outside-the-family situations.[2]

2. Feelings of insecurity. Children who feel insecure do not feel safe enough to venture forth and expose themselves to others. They lack self-confidence and self-reliance. Growing up, getting hurt, and taking social risks frighten them. This often is because of early experiences within their families where they have not been protected from feelings of embarrassment and failure. Because of their fearful attitudes, they do not develop or practice good social skills. They establish a vicious cycle of

becoming more and more shy because they do not receive positive feedback from others.

3. Overprotection. Children whose parents overprotect them from the outside world frequently are inactive and dependent and hesitant to face the world. Because their parents overprotect them, these children become quiet, passive, and shy. They have not learned to trust themselves in dealing effectively with the environment outside the family. Therefore, they see themselves as constantly needing their home and parents' protection.

When David was an infant, his mother refused to take him to Sunday school or to a Mother's Day Out program for fear he would be exposed to other children's germs. She also feared he would cry too much when she left. Therefore, David's exposure to other children—other than an occasional child in his neighborhood—was rare. As he grew older, David did not want to attend birthday parties when invited. As a school-age child, he declined to attend slumber parties and summer camps.

His mother's overprotectiveness failed to allow David to build his confidence at being apart from parents and home. It taught him instead that he could not cope adequately with the world outside the family. The result in such cases is a shy, withdrawn child.

4. Teasing. Peers, siblings, and even parents may habitually tease or ridicule children with physical disabilities or basic shyness. Such children often respond by withdrawing from others and by increasing their shyness. To avoid ridicule, these children simply avoid social contact. They become overly sensitive to being judged, rejected, or embarrassed. Particularly destructive is the ridicule of children's awkward attempts at learning to relate to others.

5. Parental harshness. Children who experience overly harsh parents begin at an early age to doubt themselves and to fear embarrassment and criticism and even physical punishment. Therefore, shyness and avoidance become their basic way of relating to the outside world.

6. Parental modeling. Shy, quiet parents often produce shy children. Living with shy adult role models not only creates

but reinforces shyness in children. Social contacts are minimal, and other people are often discussed in fearful or mistrustful terms.

Parents in many ways can help the young child minimize his or her tendency toward shyness. The counselor will find that the key in helping these young children is to work with the parents. First, parents must understand that shyness is a part of this child's inherent personality and that progress will be slow. Parents must slowly but consistently broaden their child's exposure to the outside world and at the same time provide strong and healthy positive reinforcement.

The parent-child relationship is an important one for helping a child overcome shyness. If the child experiences unconditional love and is encouraged to explore new experiences and new relationships, the child will have the self-confidence to conquer bouts of shyness.

Furthermore, parents need to teach and reward social skills. Any effort to relate to other people should be praised or rewarded in some way. While these efforts are rewarded, parents must not criticize when a child is shy or makes mistakes in social interactions. Some children respond well to praise and to rewards for less shyness and more social contact.

However, other children need to be taught social skills in order to overcome their shyness. If the child feels the parent is on his or her side and is not critical, the shyness will probably lessen. Other skills the counselor can emphasize are giving and accepting compliments, smiling, nodding, making eye contact, learning to listen, and learning to share with others. This can be a long and tedious task with the young child, but it also can be quite rewarding as the parent sees the child become less and less shy.

The child also should be exposed to supervised play or to group skills with other children the same age. Shyness can be minimized when the child has positive social experiences with his or her peers. This is only possible when these situations are supervised by adults who minimize negative interactions and encourage and reward positive interactions between the child and his or her peers.

Finally, parents also should address their own shyness if they truly want to help a child resolve his or her shyness. A counselor can help these adults develop a more positive self-esteem as they learn to trust and enjoy relationships with other adults.

THE NONAFFECTIONATE CHILD

Some of the most essential activities that contribute to bonding during infancy include holding, feeding, and cuddling. When the infant seems to resist these expressions of affection, the young parent becomes quite unsettled. While most infants do like to be cuddled, held, fed, and rocked, some seem to actively resist and seem to be constantly irritable. These same little ones seem to need constant attention and comforting. At the same time, these infants also seem never to be satisfied, no matter what efforts the parents make, creating a cycle of frustration and irritability, both in the young infant and the parent.

Furthermore, this group of children may have feeding problems: They may not be able to tolerate their formulas or breast feeding, or they may develop colic early in their lives.

Parents of these nonaffectionate children need support and reassurance with their parenting skills, since parenting to them may be a tiring and unrewarding project. These parents may need to consult frequently with a pediatrician to help with feeding problems. Careful follow-up and perhaps specific diagnostic testing may be necessary to rule out some of the biological or neurological causes of the irritable infant.

For the toddler and preschooler who seemingly are unaffectionate, more specific diagnosis may be possible. Some children have temperaments leading them to be more distant and even irritable and dysphoric in their moods. Other children, however, may have some specific problems, such as attention deficit disorder (to be discussed in chapter 15), or other developmental disorders leading to their nonaffectionate nature.

THE SLOW-TO-DEVELOP CHILD

In this section, we will review the more common areas that demonstrate delayed development; these include speech, vision, hearing, and general delayed development.

Speech

Since it is the primary way the growing child communicates with the world, speech is an important tool as the child grows and develops emotionally. One type of speech problem is the delay in speech onset. After the first year of life, speech sounds develop together with the comprehension and formulation of speech symbols. Most children begin to say their first words by about age one. The delay of the first word beyond eighteen months may indicate a serious physical, mental, or hearing problem and needs prompt professional attention.

The onset of speech frequently differs between boys and girls, with girls usually preceding boys. As speech development continues, most children by ages fourteen to twenty-four months should be able to put two words together as phrases or short sentences and will begin to use plurals as they near age two.[3]

By age thirty-six months, the child should be able to put together three-word phrases or sentences.

A delay of the onset of speech can signal a complex problem that needs evaluation by a speech pathologist and other professionals. The cause may be a specific developmental language immaturity or it may be secondary to mental retardation, serious hearing difficulties, generalized brain dysfunction, emotional disturbance—or a combination of these factors. Early evaluation and diagnosis is important because delay of speech onset can herald other communication disorders such as stuttering. It can have a profound effect on the child's emotional growth and development since one's primary means of communicating with the family is through speech and language.

Another type of speech disorder concerns articulation. A child with an articulation disorder displays immaturity of the actual formation of speech sounds by the tongue, soft palate, or lips. Articulation immaturity is seen when speech sound patterns typical of a younger child, particularly with the letters *s*, *r*, and *l*, persist well past normal time limits and when these patterns do not correct themselves without therapeutic intervention.

The Denver Articulation Screening Exam is a useful tool in which a child articulates thirty different sounds contained in twenty-two different words. The test is best administered by a professional. In general, a two-and-a-half-year-old should correctly articulate seven sounds; a four-and-a-half-year-old, eighteen sounds, and a six-and-a-half-year-old, twenty-five or more sounds.[4]

Most articulation problems concern consonants or blends, such as *th*, *ch*, and *sh*. By the time the child is in late preschool years, these difficulties may be apparent. A speech pathologist or speech therapist needs to evaluate the child.

If these articulation disorders are not corrected, the child will face increasing problems in the school setting and in relationships with peers. Language, the primary means of communicating, can be a source of ridicule if it differs from that of one's peers.

Stuttering is found in from 1 to 10 percent of the general childhood population. It is two to four times more prevalent in boys than in girls. Fifty percent of people who stutter begin before age five.[5] This is due, probably, to delayed language development skills in males. Many children pass through a phase during ages two to four when stuttering is a transient part of their speech pattern. The debate has long raged about whether this is a psychologically or an emotionally based issue.

Stuttering has many origins and many sources, but the original causes are not nearly as important as are the issues that emerge once a child has begun stuttering. This speech difficulty increases the tension in the communication process which, in turn, increases anxiety in the stuttering child. His or her anxiety then contributes to further symptoms of stuttering and language difficulties which may lead the child to avoid social situations and verbal communication, in turn, causing a delay in the child's emotional development.

The transient stuttering which many children go through between ages two and four does not call for the intervention of a speech pathologist; the problem usually resolves itself within a matter of weeks or months. However, should the stuttering persist, a speech pathologist should intervene.

Another cause of speech and language problems in children is cleft palate, a rather commonly occurring birth defect in children. A cleft palate occurs because the two sides of the soft and hard palate have failed to fuse. This may extend to involve the upper lip and causes much difficulty when the child tries to speak. Specialized treatment centers now are available to deal with the speech pathology and to offer psychological treatment such young children need, in addition to surgical correction. The earlier that intervention can occur in these children, the more normal will be the child's emotional development and speech pattern.

Vision

The child with severe visual problems or who is legally blind can be expected to have a set of special and unique concerns. Congenital or hereditary causes account for about 50 percent of blindness in younger children. A large but unknown percentage of blind children also are multiply handicapped with other problems such as cerebral palsy, epilepsy, and developmental delays.

The diagnostician should be aware of how congenital blindness (blindness since birth) impacts the child differently than does a later onset of blindness. In congenital blindness, a profound alteration in development—particularly emotional development—occurs. A child so handicapped is a high risk for serious behavior problems and severe, pervasive developmental deviation that resembles infantile autism.

Visual recognition of facial features plays a valuable role in the process of bonding between infant and mother. Bonding between the two is thus impeded when the infant is blind at birth.

This serious impairment can result in a significant "slow-down" in emotional development. It appears that it is very difficult for the young infant to bond with a mother he or she cannot see. It also appears that adults are not inclined to engage in as many social activities and bonding behaviors with blind infants and children, because of the lack of visual response, as they do with otherwise healthy offspring.

Treatment for these children is complex and requires highly specialized personnel. First, a professional must diagnose and treat the blindness, if possible. But treating the mother-child interaction is imperative as well. Treatment programs for the mother-infant bonding rely on infant stimulation programs and help develop alternate forms of communication and bonding, primarily through touch and hearing.

The young child who loses his or her vision because of disease or injury has less trouble with this bonding process. Therefore, the process of emotional development will proceed along more normal patterns. Treatment mainly centers around helping the child cope with the visual impairment. Counselors will want to advise that parents become integrally involved in the process of learning how to help the child; it may be necessary to involve professional help and/or parental support groups.

Hearing Problems

Since auditory skills also are important to the mother-infant bonding process, the child with a hearing impairment presents the therapist with yet another unique developmental situation. In such cases, more reliance is placed on the touching and visual components of the bonding process.

Since research holds that critical periods of speech and language development occur in each child, it is important that auditory deficiencies be diagnosed early. The parent should think in terms of speech and language "milestones" that are normally reached at these critical periods; if these milestones are missing, the child has more trouble obtaining them later. Some modern medical technology now exists to help with early diagnosis. Through sophisticated electronic evaluation techniques related to electroencephalograms, a technician can determine the hearing capacity of a child as young as three weeks of age.

As the child with a hearing impairment becomes older, he or she is at increased risk for behavior problems. Treatment of such problems in auditorily impaired children requires special training, not only with the help of alternative communications such as hand signing, but also training in the unique educational and social aspects of deafness.

**Generalized and Pervasive
Delays in Development**

A final type of slow-to-develop child exhibits more generalized and pervasive developmental delays. This includes the mentally retarded child. The causes of mental retardation are varied and range between genetic factors such as Down's syndrome to injuries in birth, from intrauterine accidents during pregnancy to metabolic disorders such as phenoketonuria.

Symptoms of mental retardation also are varied. They may include obvious visual, auditory, or speech impairments. Or they may manifest themselves as abnormal motor development, such as slowness in sitting up or walking. Again, early evaluation and treatment intervention with these children is imperative. This best occurs in a center that specializes in both the medical and psychological evaluation of children. Also, the center should provide infant stimulation programs, parent- and family-support programs, and specific educational interventions designed to maximize the child's cognitive and emotional development. Most communities have mental health and mental retardation programs that should be considered. The family physician can help lead parents and counselors to skilled centers.

Children who are not only mentally retarded but who also have autistic symptoms can be classed in this category of pervasive developmental disorders. Such children display varying degrees of these symptoms:

- *Their social interaction skills are impaired.* They seem to lack awareness that others exist or have feelings and fail to seek comfort during times of distress. They seem to lack interest in social interaction.
- *Their verbal and communication skills are markedly impaired.* They seem to have impaired communication ability, whether nonverbal or verbal. The child's imaginative play is absent, and they are unable to initiate or sustain any kind of verbal communication.
- They show stereotyped body movements, such as hand-flicking and finger-twisting, and seem preoccupied with small objects rather than being interested in interaction with people. They also often demonstrate marked distress when their environments change.

The cause of these autistic-type pervasive development disorders is still largely unknown. However, some experts believe the cause lies in neurological and physiological development rather than in emotional factors. These children also need highly specialized evaluation and treatment in specified centers with trained professionals. Without such treatment, they and their families are doomed to frustration and failure.

Siblings and families of children with severe developmental disabilities also need special attention. Such families are subject to chronic stress. A recent study of Breslau and Prabucki confirms that brothers and sisters of a developmentally delayed child are at high risk for developing aggressive behaviors and depressed symptoms during school-age and teen-age years.[6]

The same study confirmed that mothers and fathers of these disabled children are at increased risk for depressed symptoms. It should be clear that highly specialized therapy and support are needed for the families of these children. This seems to offer a unique opportunity for the Christian therapist who believes in the worth of the individual and the importance of the family in God's eye.

THE OPPOSITIONAL CHILD

Oppositional children (sometimes known as "brats") are those, usually under age seven, who are disruptive and difficult for parents, schoolteachers, nursery workers, Sunday school teachers, baby-sitters, and anybody and everybody to manage. It is our clinical experience that about two-thirds of all oppositional children are boys and one-third are girls.

Usually several of the following traits exist in these children:

- They have a high frequency of temper tantrums, often involving yelling, rolling on the floor, and running away.
- They are assaultive. This usually involves hitting the mother or another sibling, less frequently the father. Usually, this assaultiveness is short-lived, aimed at discouraging the parent or intimidating the younger sibling who is an innocent (or not-so-innocent) bystander.
- They demand attention, often when it is evident that such demands will embarrass the parent, disrupt the situation, or somehow be an inconvenience.

Jason, a six-year-old who could be classed as an oppositional child, only staged his tantrums when his mother was
on the telephone or had guests present, since it was difficult
for his mother to respond to him at that moment in her
normal fashion. In school, he frequently acted out when
visitors were in the classroom.

- They are defiant, often making threats. Statements such as,
  "I hate you," "I wish I could smash you," "I wish I didn't
  live here and you weren't my mother," "You're the worst
  mother in the whole world. Why don't you just go away?" "I
  don't love you at all; I hate you," are common from the
  oppositional child.
- They are overactive, although they do not demonstrate the
  classic attention deficit disorder. The oppositional child is
  often one of the most active, expressive, and physically
  mobilized children in the nursery school or Sunday school
  room.
- They anger easily. Parents often describe him or her as
  "Dr. Jekyll and Mr. Hyde." These children frequently can
  be absolutely charming in their demeanor. However, they
  can quickly become angry, accelerating into a temper
  tantrum and becoming defiant and assaultive, over seemingly incidental events. Especially incendiary to these children's emotions are events that strike at their sense of
  embarrassment or fairness, or their feeling that a parent is
  insensitive.
- They are stubborn and selfish. Holding out simply for the
  sake of holding out and being stubborn is seen in these
  children. Selfishness, especially with other siblings, is a major problem.

  Micah, six, was an oppositional child. If his mother was
  dividing candies among him and three other friends,
  Micah would balk if the other children received more
  candies than he. Micah may have just received a slice of
  apple pie, be en route to a favorite television show, and it
  may be Christmas Eve as well. But this oppositional child
  would instigate a major "fit" and temper tantrum simply
  because at that moment he came up one candy short.

A counselor achieves best results only when the parents of an oppositional child are hurting enough to solicit and stay with therapy. If parents tend to make excuses for the child's behavior, rationalize their own input, and minimize the strain that this places on themselves and on other caretakers, this reduces the likelihood of success.

We have found it best if both the father and mother seek therapy with the oppositional child. If only one parent seeks counseling, the oppositional child usually will find a way to split the parents, working around or isolating the other parent in order to reduce the consistency of efforts to help him or her change. With such children, we generally try to initiate four stages of intervention:

Phase 1—Baseline evaluation

Phase 2—Intervention

Phase 3—Reversing oppositional behavior

Phase 4—Eventual decrease of the child's "oppositional reflex" to instigating situations

Baseline Evaluation

In this phase, the child accelerates into oppositional behavior in a variety of situations. The counselor gives the parents behavioral rating sheets like the one shown in Figure 6-1. Parents take these home and assess the child's oppositional episodes. Also, the counselor spends time helping the parents develop a sense of cooperation and improved consistency in their communication.

A study by Charles Figley, professor of family therapy and psychology at Florida State University, reviewed how healthy and unhealthy families handled family problems. Families that successfully handled problems saw them as something the family had to share rather than something the parents had to struggle with alone, he found.

"Healthy families had just as many problems as did unhealthy ones, but they (healthy ones) tended to see the problem as 'ours' rather than 'yours' or 'mine,'" Figley wrote. "They took care not to put the other mate on the defensive and not to make them [sic] part of the problem, but part of the solution. Typically, one

```
Date _____

Time _____

The Situation:     _____

                   _____


The Oppositional
  Behavior:        _____

                   _____


The Parental
  Reaction:        _____

                   _____


The Outcome:       _____

                   _____
```

Figure 6–1
Behavioral Rating Sheet

spouse enlisted the help of the other in coming up with a way to cope."[7]

We suggest several key recommendations for families dealing with an oppositional child:

1. Avoid arguing in front of the child. The oppositional child will see this as an opportunity to "divide and conquer." The child, upon hearing the parents argue, can become insecure and feel that he or she is the cause of "bad family situations." The argument also assures the child that the parents do not have a united front on discipline matters; therefore, the child can zero in on some loophole in the parents' instruction.

Ron and Julie, in front of their son Justin, criticized each other about parenting decisions. Statements such as, "Why did you just let him get away with that behavior?" or "You're such a weak, ineffective father" were freely aired within full earshot of the misbehaving child. Was it any wonder, then, that Justin continued to act out in the worst possible manner?

A counselor helped Ron and Julie see that Justin would never choose positive options as long as he perceived the parents divided on his discipline. The counselor helped Ron and Julie develop some parenting skills that they could agree upon. The counselor also urged them to step aside and have a quiet, private conference on discipline matters so they could present a united front to Justin. They soon saw the child's behavior improve immensely.

2. Realize that a parent's own upbringing has much to do with how he or she appraises a child-rearing situation. Adults see any situation through the eyes of the sum of their experiences. This is especially true in home situations dealing with tough-to-solve family problems. We tend to bring a great deal of emotional "baggage" and past habits of upbringing into the situation. While some of these old habits can be useful, many are not workable under current circumstances.

When Larry was growing up, his mother's primary response to children's misbehavior was the admonition, "If you kids don't straighten up, I'll send you off to an orphanage." Although Larry, as a child, recoiled at this statement, he started to use it by force of habit when he himself was a parent. A counselor helped Larry see that threats of this nature are not helpful with children. She taught him to learn new parenting skills.

3. Learn to play to the other spouse's strengths. It may be that one reason God gives two parents to every child is because each parent at times will have better solutions to a situation than does the other parent. A parent needs to relinquish control of a situation to the other parent if it is obvious that the other parent has a better grasp of what's occurring. It's like doubles in tennis. Some shots are best taken at the net by one player whereas deeper shots can best be handled by the other player. The objective is not for one spouse to dominate situations that

arise. Rather, success in helping the oppositional child to change is what is important.

4. Use two ears and one mouth. A spouse dealing with an oppositional child may feel unappreciated and unheard by his or her mate. The counselor must see that spouses listen to one another, request the other to share feelings, and join in understanding, not criticism. Spouses who communicate with one another work out solutions that invariably are more comfortable to both.

5. Make the matter an issue of prayer. This involves the honest joining together of a husband and wife before God asking for special guidance, sensitivity, and understanding. Parents who pray together daily about a problem usually are parents who work as a single unit toward solving that problem.

Intervention

In this phase, the counselor gives the parents information about how to intervene in situations and how to change parental response. In Figure 6-2, we see how the oppositional child, using the "oppositional reflex," reacts to an escalating situation. The child is inclined to respond negatively to an escalating situation, and will establish full-fledged oppositional behavior. The oppositional behavior of the child is sure to bring a parental reaction. The outcome then often accelerates the child's oppositional behavior—if the parental reaction has not been a healthy one—and the escalating situation worsens, starting the cycle once again.

However, as parents learn intervention skills, they can convert the negative parental reaction into a positive one. The broken lines in Figure 6-3 depict how intervention skills reduce oppositional behavior, eventually deescalating the situation. Finally, these interventions are designed to decrease the child's tendency to use an oppositional reflex when encountering situations he or she does not like.

The following are five intervention skills the counselor can suggest to parents of the oppositional child:

1. "Time-outs." The parents give the child a time-out by taking the child to his or her room and insisting the child must remain there for a period of time. The time period chosen

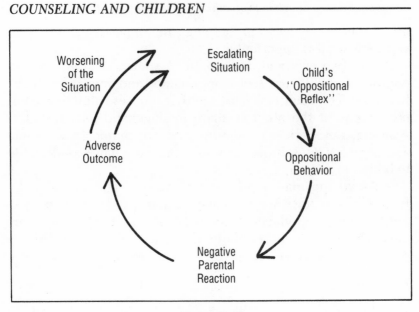

Figure 6–2

generally is consistent, and the child knows this consequence is related to oppositional behavior. The parent also can instigate a time-out by leaving the room and leaving the child alone. The latter works better if the child doesn't move easily into his or her room. A rule of thumb for the time-out is about eight minutes for each year of the child's age, with the maximum for any child being about an hour.

2. "Turn-offs." Turn-offs occur when the parents deliberately show the child no attention for a specific action. These parental "no-shows" must be practiced. Sometimes a parent can tell a four- or five-year-old child, "I'm not going to respond to you when you talk this way." The parent then either looks away or moves away, but quickly reengages the child when the parent sees even a small shift away from oppositional, or tantrum, behavior. Turn-offs seem to be especially effective with younger children who crave parental attention.

3. "Hold-downs." In this technique, the parent physically wraps his or her arms around the child to stop an oppositional or destructive behavioral escapade. The parent tells the child, "I won't let you go as long as you're acting this angry." Then the

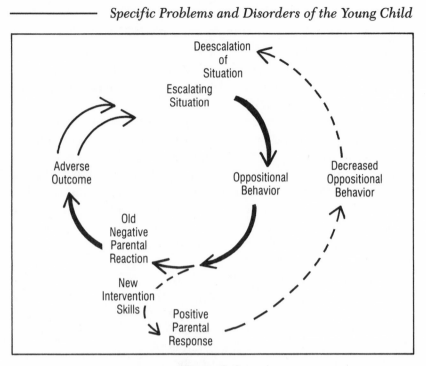

Figure 6-3

parent holds the child to decelerate the child's assaultive or aggressive behavior.

This seems to work especially well for dads, although moms also can practice the technique. "Hold-downs" actually can cut short an episode of oppositional behavior before the child is totally overwrought. As soon as the behavior begins to deescalate and the child starts to reengage the parent in a rational and more compliant fashion, the parent should respond quickly by increasing his or her attention to the child, by positive facial expressions, and some nongratuitous way of reinforcing the child's improved behavior.

4. A "consequence chart." This is a chart with two columns which the parent reviews with the child daily. In one column, the child accumulates check marks for bad attitudes or oppositional behaviors. In the other column, the child accumulates stars for good behaviors or positive attitudes. When several check marks of the first kind add up—perhaps four or five,

depending on what seems appropriate for the child—a negative consequence occurs. For example, losing the privilege to ride one's bicycle that day, having to go to bed early, or forfeiting one's favorite TV show, would be negative consequences for accumulated check marks.

5. The use of "no" and spanking, if necessary. The desirable spanking should be about four or five swats to the child's posterior without the child being injured in any way or the parent becoming hostile or aggressive. In young children, spankings can help reinforce the child's awareness that the word *no* means the parent expects an immediate change of behavior. Spanking a child who insists on running for the street, or spanking one who pummels a younger sibling can help the child learn that a physical price must be paid for insistently disobeying parents.

Spankings should never be a way for parents to ventilate their own frustrations or humiliate or intimidate the child. The child needs to understand that a bad action took place, that the spanking is the consequence for that action and that the child is not "bad." Just as the young child who touches a hot stove learns quickly from that consequence, an appropriate spanking is simply an immediate negative consequence to a behavior.

Unfortunately, because of much misunderstanding about spanking, some parents have stopped it altogether while on the other hand, some go too far and abuse the child.

Reversing Oppositional Behavior

As parents begin to use their new intervention skills, the child's oppositional behavior should decrease. This decrease normally falls into four general areas, based on the child's "goals" of misbehavior.

Goal 1—Attention Seeking. The child may have sought proofs of acceptance, approval, and significance from parents by demanding inordinate amounts of attention. If the parent supplies attention to the child when he or she is not making a bid for it, then the child will usually reduce his or her need to compete for it. The parent needs to realize that the child can get into a "dependency trap." If the child feels he or she is not significant nor appreciated by the parent, these needs to gain attention can overcome even the most effective interventions designed to reduce oppositional behavior.

We suggest that parents occasionally imagine the child saying, "Could you please notice me?" or "Do you want me? Am I special to you?" and "Are you too busy to spend time with me?" Rather than the child's having to either misbehave or struggle in some way to gain the parents' notice, the parents should adopt a more active attitude to reinforce the child's sense of worth and significance in the family.

Goal 2—Control of Power. In some family systems, maintaining and controlling power are the means by which the family parcels out worth and significance. The child struggling to gain control will give the parents the message, "You don't love me" if the child can't have his or her own way. The child will feel that only when one is in control—even if that control occurs through manipulating the parent—can one be sure of worth and value.

The parent of such a child needs to defuse "power struggles" in the home. Demonstrating to the child that no particular role in the home is of higher value than another can do this. Another way is to recognize the child's rights, but utilize parental authority consistently and effectively. Not debating or fighting back with the child when a power grab is made can also be effective. Instead, parents should let the child know limits yet validate his or her personhood. The parent should enlist the child's help and work toward cooperation rather than domination.

Counselors who encounter a home where control or power is important will be challenged to help the parents realize the effect such a mentality has on the child, and how it feeds into oppositional behavior. The parents can benefit from placing themselves in the child's position and asking themselves: "Can I be in control? Will you love me more if I am?" "Can I always have what I want? Will that always be what it takes to make me happy?" "Do you love me enough to stop me if I push you to always let me have my own way?"

Goal 3—Animosity or Revenge. Sometimes a child's goal is to misbehave in order to intimidate or pay back others for perceived injustices. The child in this situation has felt wronged or mistreated and thinks the only way to be significant or to see real hope in the situation is to retaliate. This child seeks to hurt others in order to offset feeling hurt.

In this case, the parent needs to supply the child's true need to have a "buddy," to receive encouragement, and to talk about real feelings. The child needs to observe that the parent does not become defensive or act hurt or lash out at the child. The parents should avoid harsh punishment with this type of child and should seek to win the child by kindness. Yet, in this process, the parents demonstrate to the child that they are willing to remain "in control" and to set safe limits to prevent either the child from being harmed or anyone from harming the child.

Children who feel they must retaliate in order to survive are truly set up to become oppositional children. Those who have been physically or emotionally abused, who have come from bitterly broken homes or have been victims of rejection are prone to this "goal" in misbehavior. The parent may imagine such children saying: "I want to hurt you so you'll understand why I hurt." "If I pay you back for not being there for me, then maybe you'll learn and be there for me next time." "You must hate me, so I'll drive you away from me now, so I won't have to hurt any more later on."

Goal 4—Reflection of Inadequacy. Sometimes, oppositional behavior is the child's statement that he or she feels inadequate and wants to be left alone. It's a way of driving people away from what is perceived as a hopeless situation. The child doesn't want others to see how inadequate, stupid, or "damaged" he or she is.

Ten-year-old Lanny's self-esteem suffered a major blow when his teachers moved him into a group at a lower reading level. His oppositional behavior reached a fever pitch, and he acted out by running away and physically striking at his parents repeatedly.

A counselor helped Lanny's parents understand how his sense of inadequacy had contributed to his hostile behavior. The counselor encouraged Lanny's parents to show faith in him, encouraging him and focusing on his abilities and strengths.

To be sure, parents still must intervene to deescalate the child's more negative behavior. But the underlying goal of the child's oppositional behavior is to somehow offset and escape the perceived rejection by displaying the inadequacy about himself or herself that the child feels inside. In order to understand this child better, the parent might imagine the child saying: "Would you please leave me alone? I'm not worth knowing." Or, "I feel so stupid. I hate you. You must already dislike me." And, "If I'm the worst kid around, then certainly no one will bother to take a look inside me and see how little there is in here."

Decrease in the Oppositional Reflex.

If parents are avoiding old, negative parental reactions and have begun to develop positive parental response, the child should as a result show decreased oppositional behavior, or less of the "oppositional reflex." The child will become less prone to becoming defensive, angry, hostile, and overly sensitive to rejection when situations are difficult or irritating.

The child's increasing ability to sustain appropriate behavior during situations which would previously have been overwhelming is a satisfying outcome to behold. Such personality changes don't occur over a short period of time; they may take several months to begin to surface. However, these changes are substantial in their value, not only to the child but also to the integrity and long-term health of the family unit.

It is well understood that being a part of a home that has suffered divorce impacts a child significantly. The problem is staggering in its magnitude. With a divorce rate of more than one million per year, at least one million children go through the trauma of divorce each year and more than 18 million are now living in single-parent homes.

The response of children to divorce varies with age. Children's response in the first six years of life often is marked by regression as they slide back in their development to a more dependent level. A child may begin bedwetting, may stop feeding himself or herself, or may become afraid to sleep alone.

The child of divorce suffers several adverse consequences. First of all is the loss of one parent. Additionally, divorce often brings insecurity concerning the family's ability to meet basic financial needs. The family home often cannot be maintained, so the child faces the uncertainties of relocation. Also, the child's social experience is given a jolt, for with the change of neighborhood comes a host of strange faces and loss of contact with little friends the child has known. If the mother or father chooses to remarry, the child may find that life must be shared with new family members—a new daddy or mommy, brothers and sisters.

The emotional needs of the small child are affected too, as the parent who has custody finds himself or herself overwhelmed with life in the broken home. Counselors can be most helpful to the small child by helping the parent in the home to:

- Spend quality time with God the Father in prayer.
- Tell the Lord everything, from the smallest to the most threatening problem.
- Meet with other believers regularly.
- Establish old and new friendships.
- Keep healthy.
- Do some things simply for personal enjoyment.
- Let others know about your needs.
- Tap the secrets of praise and forgiveness.
- Maintain as high a degree of financial and relationship stability as possible.
- Strive for precise predictability in visiting arrangements, holiday arrangements, and financial agreements between the divorced parents.

THE GIFTED CHILD

In modern American culture, the child who is cognitively or intellectually gifted seems more and more to be set apart as a special child needing special attention and services. While all children have certain areas in which they shine, some children clearly are intellectually gifted. At an early age they demonstrate their intellectual giftedness.

This frequently shows itself through the early development of speech and language skills, including reading, facility with math, or visual-perceptual and visual-motor skills. The latter of these reveal themselves in shows of creativity and in building skills.

The debate rages as to whether children can be taught or encouraged to be increasingly intellectually skilled, or whether there is a specific intellectual potential for each child. People often hear of infant stimulation programs designed to advance a child's intellectual and cognitive skills and make them "bright babies" even before their preschool years.

All of this occurs within a culture that appears to prize the hurried advancement of its children cognitively, socially, and emotionally. Even in the infant years, a push occurs to help our children become more productive cognitively.

A child who is intellectually gifted can be a blessing as well as a source of difficulties. Parents look on with pride as their child reaches cognitive milestones early. Yet at the same time, many of these children have difficulty in their socialization and emotional growth processes.

The counselor should keep several issues in mind when working with the family of an intellectually gifted child. The family should realize that relationships always come first. A child's cognitive ability and achievements are, indeed, important, but they are not as important as is the development of healthy, strong relationships with parents and siblings. Upon the family relationships all future relationships will be based. While parents should encourage the child's cognitive development by playing special games and enrolling him or her in advanced educational programs, none of these activities can take the place of the parents' playing with, holding, loving, and cuddling a child.

The family should remember that children who are gifted intellectually still have age-appropriate emotional and social needs. It is easy to think of these children as being older than they are and therefore to ignore some of their basic emotional needs. When this occurs, important emotional milestones may go unmet, and the child may be at risk for unhappiness and perhaps emotional development troubles later in life.

Carson began studying the violin at age three and the piano at age four. By the time he was in first grade, Carson was amazingly skilled on both instruments, and he played private recitals for the suburban community where he lived. His music studies required him to practice four hours a day, leaving him no time to play with friends after school. One day he announced to his parents that he was through with both instruments. During the counseling that ensued, Carson's parents were helped to see that the youngster still had the emotional needs of a first grader even though his musical skills were that of a much older child. His parents worked to adjust his practice time to allow periods for after-school play and socialization.

The family should remember that intellectually gifted children are at high risk of becoming "overachievers" later in life. Because of the value society places on intellectual ability, it is easy for the child to learn that life is based on how much he can produce or how much he can perform. Therefore, much energy will be spent in trying to achieve and overachieve in order to develop a sense of personal self-worth and self-esteem. The family should emphasize that relationships and emotional needs are important in the child's growing up.

Lastly, the family should remember that children who have intellectual giftedness frequently have parents who themselves are overachievers and who seek ways to perform and produce in order to develop their own self-worth. Such parents also need to watch their tendency toward overachievement and perfectionism.

Families of gifted children frequently need help in learning how to play together and how to relax together and to enjoy each other's company rather than being totally focused on achievement.

Christian parents will want to focus especially on the fact that their gifted child is a special and unique creation God has entrusted to them. Opportunities within the church and the family will encourage the child to use his giftedness in service of Christ. Such opportunities may include Bible memory, expression in the Christian arts (music, drama, art, and writing). The gifted child also needs to hear clearly the parents' gratitude to God for the special gifts placed in that child.

The gifted child and his family face unique challenges. While there is much excitement in watching the gifted child explore and use special abilities, that child and the family must also be careful to thank the Heavenly Father for those special gifts and talents. Patience, understanding, and love expressed to other children as well as a sense of camaraderie with peers are essential in avoiding the loneliness that gifted children often experience. In God's sight, indeed, all children are created equal. Special gifts or talents are given by the grace of God. Children should be carefully guided in their stewardship of these gifts in order to glorify God, not to glorify the child or his or her family.

CHAPTER SEVEN

THE CHILD WITH EMOTIONAL DISORDERS

THE CHILD UNFOLDS IN PERSONALITY much as a rosebud slowly unfolds petal by petal, into a full-blossomed flower. Conduct which may be appropriate at ages four and five, for example, would be highly inappropriate at ages eighteen or nineteen. The fantasies and thought constructions of a three-year-old are odd and interesting but absolutely normal; yet the same thought processes in a twelve-year-old are thought to indicate a psychopathological disorder.

Anyone actively counseling children will see these various disorders from time to time, although counselors who do not have specialized training in these syndromes should not attempt to treat such clients.

The following eight categories represent an overview of the major psychopathological disorders of childhood:
1. Developmental disorders
2. Disruptive behavior disorders*
3. Anxiety disorders*
4. Eating disorders
5. Gender-identity disorders
6. Stereotyped movement disorders
7. Adjustment disorders and depression
8. Special symptoms and other disorders

In this chapter we will discuss these and their implications for counselors of small children.

DEVELOPMENTAL DISORDERS

Mental Retardation

Mental retardation is characterized by below-average intellectual functioning. In the young child, intelligence (IQ) tests are not as reliable or as valid as they are in older children, so a general clinical assessment of the child's developmental milestones and the age-appropriateness of those milestones is used to assess intellectual development.

The concern for mental retardation would be addressed by trying to determine how appropriate the child's behavior is in social settings, how developed are the child's interpersonal skills, and how well the child communicates with words and phrases.

Other areas of concern would be: how well the child carries out basic living skills, how well he or she ambulates and shows fine motor skills at the appropriate points, and the degree to which progressively more sophisticated communications are understood.

As the child grows older and intelligence can be measured through IQ readings, it becomes helpful to consider retardation in two areas: primary and secondary retardation.

Primary retardation applies to those individuals with

---

*Disruptive behavior disorders, including attention deficit, are discussed in detail in chapters 14 and 15. Anxiety disorders are also discussed in chapter 12, under the subject, "The Fearful and Anxious Child."

full-scale IQ levels of between 50 and 70. These individuals generally show no acute physical abnormalities, neurological handicaps, or other congenital deficits that are immediately apparent to others. Alternate terms for primary retardation have been residual retardation, endogenous retardation, aclinical retardation, and cultural-familial retardation.

Individuals with primary retardation have a general absence of discernible brain pathology. Environmental and possibly hereditary factors appear to be equally significant in the formation of primary retardation.

Secondary retardation reflects a level of intellectual functioning which can be moderate (IQ 35 to 49), severe (IQ 20 to 34), or profound (IQ under 20). In most cases, these individuals have brain disease, or some structural injury to the brain's functioning has caused retardation. Such injuries frequently are accompanied by some physical handicap, neurological deficit, or congenital malformation.

Several categories of disorders are known to cause primary or secondary retardation. They are:

1. Infections and toxic states. This includes infections such as rubella, toxoplasmosis, congenital syphilis, postnatal cerebral infection, hyperbilirubinemia, fetal alcohol syndrome, cytomegalic inclusion disease (CID), encephalopathies due to intoxication (such as lead intoxication), or postimmunization encephalopathy.

2. Hypoxia or physical trauma. This includes injury at birth from a difficult or traumatic labor and delivery, prenatal injury, or perinatal hypoxia (resulting from an interruption of the oxygen supply to the brain during birth, such as caused by the umbilical cord being wrapped around the baby's neck).

3. Nutritional or metabolic disorders. The brain's inability to metabolize its own natural chemicals or to nutritionally function properly can cause mental retardation. A detailed explanation of these is a fairly sophisticated matter medically and is beyond the scope of this book. More detailed information is available from a pediatrician, a family practitioner, or the March of Dimes office. Several of these disorders are: Tay-Sachs disease, Niemann-Pick's disease, Gaucher's disease, the mucopolysaccharidoses, Hurler's syndrome, Hunter's syndrome, the lipid disorders, and

various carbohydrate disorders (e.g., Von Gierke's disease and hypoglycemia). Amino acid disorders, such as phenylketonuria, also can cause mental retardation, as can minimal metabolic disease (e.g., Wilson's disease) and endocrine diseases (e.g., hypothyroidism [cretinism]).

4. Major anatomical brain disorders. This includes tuberous sclerosis, Sturge-Weber disease, neurofibromatosis, and a variety of demyelinating diseases.

5. Idiopathic (or unknown) causes of malformations, including hydrocephalus, macrocephaly, craniostenosis, congenital porencephaly, and microgyria.

6. Chromosomal abnormalities. These are causes of retardation having to do with the injury or malfunction of the forty-six chromosomes. The most common of these is Down's syndrome, although others exist, such as the short-arm deletion of chromosome five and X and Y chromosome abnormalities. An evaluation by a trained geneticist can diagnose chromosomal abnormalities.

7. Disorders of gestation. This pertains to babies born prematurely and who may suffer harm because of inadequate development at birth.

8. Retardation secondary to severe sensory deprivation. Young children exposed to prolonged isolation, such as those locked in a closet for long periods of time and who are unable to see or hear, can have retarded intellectual development.

Pervasive Developmental Disorders

These disorders include autism, childhood schizophrenia, and symbiotic psychosis.

Autism usually shows itself before thirty months of age and is accompanied by a variety of signs, including a major disturbance of language development, a pervasive lack of response to other people in the environment, and incoherence and bizarre responses to surroundings—such as extreme resistance to change or a major attachment to things. *The Diagnostic and Statistical Manual–III–Revised* of the American Psychiatric Association (DSM–III–R) gives sixteen items seen in autism. Eight are required to make the diagnosis.

In contrast to autism, childhood schizophrenia usually is first diagnosed sometime above kindergarten age. These children may show true disturbances in thought organization, with auditory or visual hallucinations and frank delusions. Their speech may be bizarre and their behavior odd as well. Unlike the autistic child, they may attempt to use speech to communicate, but their speech frequently is bizarre in its construction and contains neologisms (new, or made-up, words).

The symbiotic psychosis essentially is a psychotic reaction occurring in a child placed in a situation where he or she must function somewhat separately or autonomously from the parents. In that situation, the child can become psychotic, with confusion, panic, and strange behaviors.

Specific Developmental Disorders

The specific developmental disorders show an impairment in only one or a few areas of development, unlike the pervasive disorders, which showed a marked diminishing of function in a wide variety of areas. These disorders include the areas of language, reading, and "clumsiness" (developmental coordination disorder). Various learning disorders also come under this category.

EATING DISORDERS

The eating disorders fall roughly into five categories, anorexia nervosa being the most commonly known of them. Anorexia nervosa and bulimia generally are problems of the adolescent and older and need not be discussed in this book.

The third eating disorder of childhood, pica, is the persistent eating of items that are not food—cloth, plaster, paint, and dirt. It must be diagnosed over a period of at least a month and may not be due to any other mental disorder. The exact cause of pica is not known; some nutritionists consider it a mineral deficiency or, at times, a reaction to severe neglect.

Rumination disorder, a fourth eating problem, takes its name from the fact that children will regurgitate food, rechew it, and swallow it much as a cow ruminates and chews its cud. The diagnosis requires that the child has lost weight or not reached his or her expected weight. This disorder also must be associated with at least one month of repeated regurgitation without identifiable gastrointestinal illness. Nausea is usually absent, and the child seems irritable and hungry between episodes of regurgitation. This is a serious disorder and should be treated by a specialist; there is a significant mortality rate with this.

Finally, we have the category of unspecified eating disorders. These include the unusual disorder of psychogenic dwarfism. Unlike the traditional dwarfism which is genetically determined, in this disorder the pituitary gland, which is key to a child's growth, ceases to function adequately in response to psychological stress, particularly abandonment and neglect by the parents. Other unspecified eating disorders include severe pickiness and a proclivity to limit one's diet to particular food preferences or "food fads," to the exclusion of other normal nutrition.

GENDER-IDENTITY DISORDERS

Gender-identity disorders occur in an individual who feels intense distress about his or her sex. An example is a young girl who repeatedly says that her desire is to be a boy but does not state any perceivable social or cultural advantages. She also displays an aversion to normal female clothing and female-oriented toys. She appears to reject her own female anatomy and sometimes refuses to sit while urinating, asserting that she will grow a penis; in adolescence, she may not want to acknowledge any growth in breast size.

Young males with this disorder display an intense anguish about being male and a strong desire to be a girl. Preoccupied with female activities, they shun stereotyped male activities and repudiate their male anatomy. They express the desire to grow up one day and become a woman and are repulsed by penises and testicles, stating they would rather not be anatomically so formed.

Other gender-identity disorders occur when a child persistently dresses as a member of the opposite sex but does not demonstrate the other criteria for a major gender-identity disorder. The American Psychiatric Association no longer considers homosexuality a psychopathological condition. However, normal gender identification is disrupted if a child is consistently fascinated with sexual intimacy with a member of the same sex and has an obsessional inability to change that attraction.

Sexual curiosity, whether about members of one's own or the opposite sex, is rather common in children, and in preteens as well. By adolescence, curiosity begins to form along lines of primary interest in members of the opposite sex, with less and less attraction sexually to members of the same sex.

Because a young boy or girl has had an episode of homosexual behavior, or acts out some homosexual curiosity, no one should conclude that the child will become homosexual in lifelong sexual preference. Although homosexual behavior may have some genetic weighting, the early life experiences of the young boy or girl are the primary factors which go into shaping normal or abnormal identification.

STEREOTYPED MOVEMENT DISORDERS

The stereotyped movement disorders include a transient tic disorder. Intermittent, rapid, purposeless, muscle contractions carried out in an involuntary fashion, tics are often distressing; the child almost always feels some shame and self-consciousness. They are frequently transient. That is, they come and go in children. The tics sometimes are called "typical" stereotyped movements; atypical stereotyped movements are voluntary and sometimes pleasurable. Headbanging is one of these.

Transient tic disorder is a type of tic involving the face, such as a wink or eye blink. The tic may include limbs or even vocalizations. The most common kind is Tourette's disorder, which affects one in about ten thousand youngsters. The symptoms normally begin between the ages of eight and thirteen. In about half the cases, a single simple tic, such as a twitch or an eye blink, occurs. Often other voluntary movements, such as grunts, snorts, yelps, hopping, and squatting, occur.

The atypical stereotyped disorders of movement are those such as rocking back and forth or head banging, which can be seen superimposed upon other disorders such as sensory deprivation, autism, and mental retardation. These are usually outgrown as a person moves into adulthood.

ADJUSTMENT DISORDERS AND DEPRESSION

Adjustment disorders of childhood are maladaptive or poorly adaptive adjustments to some major stress, whether psychological, physical, or social. Children as a group are more vulnerable to adjustment disorders than are adults, because children are less mature and less experienced in dealing with crises and have less mental and physical strength than adults.

Adjustment disorders occur in healthy children. Symptoms can be changes in bowel habits, bladder habits, social adaptation, emotional stability, school performance, confidence with others, interest in activities, sleep, and appetite. These disturbances should abate within three months of the stressing incident and usually do not reappear unless the stressor continues.

Depression also can occur in the child. It often presents itself in other-than-typical fashion for children—not always with the sadness, discouragement, and sense of hopelessness that adults often verbalize. Childhood depression is discussed extensively in chapter 12. Depression is probably under-recognized and under-treated in children. Thirty to 50 percent develop major depression by age 17, if one parent has major depression. These depressions usually last between 7 and 8 months, and 15 to 20 percent of children may not recover by 2 years from onset. The risk of relapse of depression after recovery is over 50 percent. Since the 1950s, the rate of suicide in children and adolescents has tripled. The message in these statistics is that the depressed child needs to be aggressively treated, not overlooked.[1]

"Youngsters with major depression or dysthymia," says Maria Kovacs, "will recover from the episode of disturbance for which they were referred for treatment. However, they may show residual impairment in social functioning and their educational process and learning may be slowed down as well."[2]

Childhood schizophrenia was discussed earlier in the section on developmental disorders. However, to reiterate, schizophrenia can occur in children and often shows disorganized thought, bizarre speech and behavior, delusions, and auditory or visual hallucinations. The schizophrenic child initially may seem particularly irritable, often confused and disturbed by changes in his or her environment. These children may isolate themselves in a fantasy world. In time, their sheer panic and discouragement becomes evident, and hallucinations and delusional fears may surface.

SPECIAL SYMPTOMS AND OTHER DISORDERS

These disorders include functional enuresis (bedwetting) and functional encopresis (soiling). Enuresis is one of the most common problems of early childhood. The prevalence of bedwetting in children at age 4 exceeds about 10 percent. By age 5, it decreases to about 7 percent in boys and 3 percent in girls. Then it tapers down as the child grows older.

The most common cause is a lack of maturation in the bladder development in terms of physiological function and neurological enervation. Enuresis occurring after a period of being dry (called secondary enuresis) is more likely to be psychological in origin, although certain disorders, such as diabetes or seizures or other infections, need to be ruled out. Later in this chapter, in "Problems in Bodily Functions," we discuss enuresis and encopresis more thoroughly.

Sleep disorders, which also can occur in childhood, include sleep terror disorder, sleepwalking, and nightmares. Sleep terror disorder usually begins between ages four and twelve and may involve an abrupt awakening for one to ten minutes. This often is preceded by a scream of panic and intense anxiety. The child shows intense arousal, including rapid breathing, dilated pupils, sweating, and rapid heart rate.

Nightmares, on the other hand, or bad dreams, show milder anxiety. The child does not awake with a start and screaming. Children often recall nightmares afterward, whereas they often do not remember night terrors.

Sleepwalking disorder usually begins between ages six and twelve and involves the child rising at night and walking for several minutes. The child often does not remember what happened during the episode. The child may not awaken easily during somnambulism, but once the child awakens, he or she generally has normal mental functioning.

Stuttering, elective mutism, and cluttering are other special symptoms in childhood. Stuttering involves frequent repetition of words, or repetition between syllables as the child struggles to overcome a barrier in fluency. On the other hand, cluttering disrupts the flow and rhythm of speech, making speech hard to understand. It involves jerky and sometimes rapid spurts of phrases that don't naturally flow together well in rhythm.

Elective mutism is a refusal to speak in most situations, such as at school. The child actually has the ability to speak and to comprehend the spoken language. However, the child elects to control his or her environment through body language such as nods, gestures, and even one-syllable words. This is one of the few disorders that occurs slightly more frequently in girls than in boys. The problem generally ends after a few weeks to several months, but if parents reinforce it greatly by showing too much attention, the symptom may persist longer.

The schizoid disorder of childhood is manifested by poor ability in social relations without any observable link to any other disorder. The schizoid child is considered a loner and is content to be so, has few close friends, and avoids peer contact.

Although serious mental disorders definitely affect young children, thankfully, these are much less common than are the majority of other disorders discussed in this book. The counselor's main goal is to recognize general symptoms of these disorders, reassuring the parents that treatment exists and referring the parents to competent professional help.

The Child with Habits

Although thumb-sucking is quite common in the first and second years of life, the incidence of it gradually declines with advancing age in children. Approximately 40 percent of all 1-year-olds, 20 percent of 5-year-olds, and 5 percent of 10-year-olds actively suck their thumbs.[3]

Thumb-sucking seems pleasurable, restful, and relaxing for the child; children also turn to it when they are anxious, scared, hungry, or generally feel threatened. In general, we have found that those who suck their thumbs are no more emotionally disturbed than are other children. Dentists do warn that thumb-sucking, especially beyond the fifth year, increases the risk of dental and facial malformations.

How to treat this habit can be controversial, and the methods are certainly varied. For the child under five, it is generally best to ignore thumb-sucking and see it only as a developmental phase through which the child soon will pass. But if the habit persists and becomes a problem, parents can begin a program to help the child stop.

The first step in that program is to give the child a time and place when thumb-sucking is permissible, for example, at bedtime or naptime. At other times, parents can give the child a gentle reminder that sucking is not appropriate and that the child must stop the activity. While this may not halt the thumb-sucking entirely, this approach may limit it drastically.

Measures such as bandaging the thumb, using unpleasant tasting "paints," and other such negative interventions usually are not necessary and may be counterproductive. If a child has this habit because he or she is afraid or insecure, the thumb-sucking most likely will not stop unless the root problem is addressed. This requires patience, the emphasizing of a positive relationship between parent and child, and by giving the child permission to thumb-suck at specific times and places.

Generally, parents should remember that time is on their side. Most children will stop on their own without much parental intervention.

Nail-biting, another problem frequently seen in the young child, particularly among four- and five-year-olds, usually indicates anxiety more than does thumb-sucking. During fearful or scary times, some children will chew on their fingernails. These children have well-bitten nails and, frequently, sore fingertips because of this habit.

To treat this problem, parents should keep the child's nails trimmed and filed so that no rough edges show. Smooth nails are harder to bite than ragged and rough-edged ones. Nagging, shaming, or scolding the child about nail-biting is more likely to aggravate and increase the habit than to help it. The parent should discuss with the child feelings he or she may be expressing and try to increase the child's motivation to stop. This can be done by giving simple rewards for having unbitten nails or by helping the child learn to verbalize his or her feelings of anxiety and fear rather than biting one's nails.

A related type of habitual behavior in young children is hair-pulling, described in the medical literature as trichotillomania. Frequently, this is related to young children's anxiety and insecurity. During waking hours, they may pull or twist their hair. More oppressive, though, is the nighttime behavior of these children. While asleep, they twist and pull and sometimes even eat their hair. This will cause patches of baldness about the child's scalp, particularly in areas that are easily accessible to the child's fingers.

Frequently, this problem becomes so severe that these young children must wear caps during the day to cover their patches of baldness. The practice of eating the hair puts the child at risk medically. Hair is poorly digested; inside the stomach, it forms a ball called a bezoar. At times, these bezoars need to be removed surgically.

Treatment for hair-pulling is aimed at decreasing the child's anxiety. This may be done by increasing play time with parents and by parents talking with their child about his or her feelings of anxiety. The therapist should look for any type of stress in the family, particularly marital stress. The child may need to wear mittens to bed so that pulling the hair becomes more difficult to do. Parents should monitor the child's behavior, being alert for chronic abdominal pain or persistent vomiting in case the child has developed a bezoar as described above.

The Overindulged Child

Overindulged or spoiled children are sometimes described as children who feel they are entitled to everything they want and who feel delays are unacceptable. Karen Schuman, a New York-based Parent Effectiveness Training instructor, calls the spoiled child "one who gets everything—except what he really needs."[4] The primary mark of the spoiled child is usually a series of telltale, overindulgent parental behaviors. Some of these are:

1. The parent gives *things* as a substitute for emotional involvement or quality time. This may occur because the parent is uncomfortable with dealing intensely with the child. The parent may be selfish and act in a self-centered manner. Or, the parent may feel inadequate to meet the child's emotional needs. Therefore, because of parental guilt, the child is overindulged.

2. Parents overindulge because of societal or peer pressure. The old adage, "keeping up with the Joneses," may be

overused, yet it reflects some of the pressure parents feel. They may feel pressured to keep their children dressed in the height of fashion, or to provide children with the latest gadgets reflecting parental affluence, or to send their children to all the "right places" with money to spend.

3. Parents attempt to use material goods as a form of emotional anesthetic with the child. When marital conflict or emotional or situational pressure occurs in the home, parents may distract or anesthetize children with material items. This is similar to adults overindulging themselves with food to mask emotional pain or frustration. Overindulgence with material goods can evade emotional rejection or avoid conflict.

4. Parents overindulge to compensate for their own childhood deprivations or personal unhappiness, aiming to give their children a better upbringing environment than they enjoyed themselves. Unfortunately, material overindulgence sometimes becomes a way for parents to placate their children and inadvertently to spoil them.

5. Parents overindulge to compensate for feeling that they have been too harsh or restrictive on their children. Sometimes parents feel their religious or personal philosophies have caused them to limit their children from many otherwise enjoyable activities. They feel that giving the children expensive material goods will make up for their limitations. Sometimes parents find it easier to give things as an alternative gratification rather than explain in detail why certain of the child's wishes are curtailed.

6. Parents may simply give out of generosity, without any bad motives. But while their intentions are worthy, sometimes such overindulgence can adversely affect the child.

Overindulgence can cause children to respond in several ways:

1. They often jump from project to project and have trouble completing activities which do not deliver immediate gratification. The overindulged child tends to have little patience with lengthy endeavors requiring perseverance.

2. Overindulged children often are overly influenced by peer pressure. They have a profound need for others' approval and feel they sometimes need to buy friendships or have things

to be "fun" and acceptable. This makes them susceptible to the wishes and control of others. These children often grow to be unhappy with themselves and have a chronic lack of inner contentment.

3. They often are not sensitive to others' needs. This compassionless lack of empathy is fueled by the repeated stimulation their selfish side gets from the regular flow of "goodies."

4. Overindulged children unfortunately develop a poor sense of appreciation and respect for their possessions. The ability to properly care for an item, to keep it in working order, and to extract long-term use from it is hard for overindulged children. They unconsciously ask themselves, *why should I bother taking care of this? If it breaks, wears out, or I lose it, something just as good or better quickly will be provided me.*

5. They also tend to be impulsive and exercise poor judgment in the area of finances. Their parents often give them money. They are without realistic chores or a predictable allowance for which they have certain responsibilities. Adults with an "easy come, easy go" attitude toward finances often were poorly trained with regard to money in their early years.

6. Overindulged children may be prone to deceitfulness and a tendency to manipulate others. To these children, material goods are never totally satisfying; nor are material goods ever adequate, since someone always has something a little better. The child who seeks to build self-esteem with material goods readily swings into a pattern of deceitfulness and into telling half-truths. It has been said that oversaturating a child with toys and privileges "softens the conscience."

7. Finally, they often struggle with the concept of performance and achievement. Because they have been rewarded capriciously and extensively, they often are caught between wishing to provide handily for themselves and fearing they do not have the true skills and persistence required to maintain such a lifestyle. They have a sense of entitlement, yet they become frustrated at their own lack of tough discipline and fear they are not equipped to truly provide for themselves.

When faced with an overindulged or spoiled child, the counselor should assist the parent in making constructive changes in the following areas:

1. Parents should develop a hard-work ethic at home, with clear expectations and responsibilities for the child. They should arrange a fair level of monetary compensation for the work the child does. This will help the child develop a sense of responsibility.

2. Parents should join the child in cooperative efforts, working side-by-side to attain goals—and not only start but finish projects together. It is helpful for the child to have the model of parents expressing a healthy respect for hard work and persistence.

3. Parents themselves should demonstrate a lack of personal slavery to material goods. They should demonstrate they are not overly influenced by the pressure to maintain an affluent lifestyle or to keep up appearances with others by obtaining material goods. The family that stresses personal values, a sense of family heritage, and spiritually sound training rather than the incessant pursuit of materialism will build depth into the child.

4. Parents should teach the overindulged child about service to and compassion for others. They should teach the concept of sharing with others and of making personal and material sacrifices so that others may benefit. They should also follow through on commitments to help in such activities as church outreach projects, and through community assistance programs for the indigent through agencies such as United Way.

5. Parents should seek to enhance the level of creativity in their child by teaching the child to entertain himself or herself, with little outside stimulation, and to be content with little. Limiting television viewing, especially programs appealing to the more base elements of the child's personality, is a good way to encourage the child toward creative activities. Participation in team sports, community activities, and church functions helps the child with interpersonal relationships.

6. Parents should allow the child to experience the consequences of his or her own actions. The parent who always intervenes to help the child with homework actually encourages the child to continue a sense of entitlement. This also applies to the parent who attempts to straighten out interpersonal conflicts the child gets into or who constantly picks up the child's stray toys or possessions.

7. Parents should strive to be consistent, less willing to give in to the child's demands, and to say no to some of the latest fads. Parents who are a "soft touch," who seem to regularly give in to the child's demands, may need the support and intervention of a counselor if the child is using psychological manipulation to get what he or she wants. Miami child psychologist Tiffany Fields says: "If one parent is being excessively authoritative and the other is excessively permissive, sometimes this balances out and doesn't disturb the child, as long as they [parents] disagree privately and still maintain a united front. Otherwise the child will often manipulate the permissive parent."[5]

Problems with Bodily Functions

The young child may demonstrate problems in body functions, including everything from eating problems to soiling and sleep difficulties. Unlike the ones previously discussed—bedwetting, eating disorders, etc.—these affect behavior but do not necessarily represent emotional disturbance.

Eating problems especially concern the parents of infants. Debate continues as to whether children are best served by breast-feeding or bottle-feeding. Research seems to indicate that both methods provide adequate nutrition. While some enhanced bonding occurs during breast-feeding, adequate bonding certainly can occur even if a mother chooses to bottle-feed her infant. The ultimate decision for the method chosen lies with the mother.

Those surrounding the mother must take care not to make her feel guilty because of the choice she makes. Besides some enhancement of bonding, breast-feeding's advantage is providing some natural immunoglobulins via the mother's breast milk that are not available in the bottled formulas. The disadvantages of breast-feeding are its inconvenience and the inability of the father to participate frequently in the feeding process. Formula-feeding is adequate nutritionally for children. Modern formulas are highly researched and are well-balanced sources of nutrition.

Feeding problems in infancy include frequent spitting-up episodes or diarrhea. This may require multiple visits to the pediatrician's office to determine changes to be made in feeding or in formula. The mother's anxiety level can increase during these times. The father should support the mother as she tries to find the correct formula and feeding pattern for her baby.

Colic also is a common problem occurring early in infancy. The child seems to have almost inscrutable abdominal cramps. Although doctors have studied the problem, no clear answers exist for cause and treatment. Colic generally subsides by age three to four months. Frequently, children who later are diagnosed as having attention deficit disorder are found to have had feeding problems, including colic.

The parents can be reassured by the fact that children eventually outgrow colic. Doctors should advise only the occasional use of medication to cut down on the child's seeming abdominal cramps.

Food allergies are a common feeding problem and can cause symptoms all the way from vomiting and diarrhea to behavior changes. Careful follow-up from a pediatrician is necessary to help identify and treat the child with specific food allergies.

As the child becomes older, feeding problems become generally centered around the level of the child's appetite and around his or her preoccupation with one type of food at the expense of trying new foods. Parents should plan nutritional meals for their children but should avoid power struggles about what is to be eaten. They will expect children to try different and new foods and not to like all foods.

Toilet training: Here, parents must avoid being lax and indifferent but also must not be overly punitive. The process of toilet training naturally is anxiety-producing for most children. Overly punitive methods of trying to enforce toilet training simply increase the child's anxiety and fear, making the task more difficult.

Parents can try many different toilet-training plans. All of them have the same basic approach. First, parents should decrease the anxiety associated with the child's beginning to use the toilet. This means helping the child begin to use the toilet. Some parents richly reward toileting successes with star charts or other means of gratification. However, they will not want to respond harshly to mistakes.

According to Gesell's developmental milestones, the child by fifteen months is usually standing and may squat in order to defecate. He or she may enjoy walking to the toilet, especially with positive attention from the parents, but he or she cannot delay voluntary defecation. When speech begins sometime before twenty-four months, the child can communicate verbally the need for toileting, but he or she still may have trouble learning that soiling outside the toilet is socially unacceptable. A child at this age also may enjoy playing with the feces.

By age three, the child can postpone defecation voluntarily and can ask for help in toileting. By age four, toilet training is generally complete and the child no longer requires parental assistance. Although adult-like toileting behavior usually occurs by age four, interest in size, color, shape, and consistency of feces frequently remains high past this age.[6]

Nocturnal enuresis (bedwetting) is common in very young children. In fact, bedwetting is not considered out of the range of normal behavior until the child reaches about five or six years of age. Probably because of their relative delay in maturity as compared to girls, boys have a higher frequency of nocturnal enuresis than do girls.

The counselor should encourage parents not to be overly punitive when the very young child has nocturnal enuresis. Instead, parents should show support, consistency, and love to these children, since most of them will resolve their problems with enuresis by the time they reach school age. (A larger discussion of enuresis is in chapter 14.)

Encopresis, or fecal soiling, is another problem in the young child under age four, even after toilet training is complete. Frequently, the child soils his or her underwear because he or she retains stool due to fear, power struggles, or pain in having a bowel movement. Retention of stool causes some feces to leak around the large plug of retained feces. Therefore, the pants are soiled. Treatment of this problem soiling also is discussed in chapter 14.

Sleep problems: Children need adequate sleep, not only so the child's body can function properly but also for the child's psychological well-being. Adequate sleep also is important for the psychological well-being of the parents.

Mild sleep disturbances are common in childhood, especially at ages two to five years. Normally, these disturbances are reactions to the insecurities of growing up. They occur primarily when the child wakes in the middle of the night, crying or seeking to be in bed with the parents. Disturbing dreams and restlessness in sleep are the two most common sources of these problems. Although mild and temporary sleep disturbances occur commonly in childhood, severe and/or persistent sleep difficulties often are the early signs of serious emotional disturbances. The underlying causes of sleep disturbances in the young child are many, including anxiety, internal conflicts, physical sleep disorders, overstimulation, fear of the dark, and situational or family stress.

For many young children, sleep is like an actual separation from parents. Many sleep disturbances are linked to this kind of anxiety. Children often actually fear something will happen to their parents while they sleep.

Recent sleep research has established that sleep is cyclical in nature. During sleep time, the child goes in and out of four different stages of sleep. After emerging from the deepest sleep stage, rapid eye movements (REM) sleep usually occurs, during which time vivid dream activity happens. Studies of sleepwalking, sleeptalking, night terrors, and bedwetting show these disorders often occur during sudden and intense arousal from deep sleep stages and are not related to REM sleep.[7] The disorders just mentioned are actually called disorders of sleep arousal.

Narcolepsy, or excessive sleepiness, on the other hand, is associated with the abnormal occurrence of REM sleep. Disorders of arousal of sleep are most often associated with signs of neurologic immaturity. Furthermore, sleep arousal disorders rarely occur in a family pattern. Before sleep research and sleep studies in children became highly sophisticated, these arousal disturbances were commonly considered to be caused by bad dreams. The specific and actual causes, however, of these sleep arousal disorders are still poorly understood.

Specific sleep disorders are treated in various ways, as the following demonstrates.

Colic and other physical causes of sleeplessness. Teething frequently is mentioned as a cause of sleep problems in young infants and toddlers. Its importance is probably overestimated. However, colic certainly may cause sleep disturbances in the very young infant.

Since colic generally is gone by age three to four months, the main concern is not with colic per se but with patterns learned as the parents try to deal with colic during those early months. Parents make extensive efforts to make the baby more comfortable. They rock the baby, walk the floor, and pat the baby on the back for countless hours. Unfortunately, when the colic disappears, the behavior patterns, particularly at nighttime, may persist. The baby may not easily fall asleep again. Successful treatment requires simply establishing or reestablishing a healthy bedtime routine of sleep onset behaviors.

Fears of the dark and other anxieties. Sometimes sleep problems occur in young children if the child is anxious and has a multitude of fears of the dark or other specific things. Bad dreams may trigger these, but frequently they don't. Childhood fears are common, particularly in the preschooler, age four to six. We know these fears are a way, through projection, that the child copes with many angry and aggressive impulses that children of this age have.

Associated with these fears can be an active dream and even nightmare experience. Managing these childhood fears which occur primarily at night involves assurance to the child that Mom and Dad are present, warm, caring, and protective. This does not mean the parent remains in the room. In fact, that would be undesirable management.

The parent who tries to prove that the child has nothing to fear will find that method fails. The child's fears are very real and nothing can persuade the child that those fears don't exist. Instead, the parent should be firm but protective, allowing the child to experience the fact that fears are part of life but can be overcome. Therefore, the parent may need to go with the child to the bedroom and stay for a few minutes as the child becomes comfortable and falls asleep.

However, the parent should not spend the night in the child's room or allow the child to sleep with the parents. This intervention actually teaches the child that some things are so fearful that the child cannot cope with them. Similarly, parents should avoid the unintentional reinforcement of the child's fears. When a parent spends time shining lights in closets or looking through drawers or out windows to make sure no monster exists, the parent is actually admitting that the monster possibly exists.

In summary, then, the parent who deals with the young child's fears should approach the child with reassurance, firmness, and protectiveness. Attempts to uncover the subconscious origins of the child's fear generally fail.

Delayed sleep phase. Some children, for reasons that do not seem clear, have much trouble falling asleep at night. Sleep studies for even young children are available in major medical centers, and children who are affected by sleep troubles probably should be evaluated. The children in this category have a "delayed sleep phase" wherein they can achieve a normal amount of sleep, but sleep for them begins and ends a few hours later than is customary or desired by the parents. It seems the child falls asleep at the same late hour night after night, regardless of the actual bedtime or parental demands.

The exact hour of sleep coincides with the child's physiological readiness for sleep rather than with the family's intentions. Parents can adjust the timing of the sleep cycle as part of the treatment process. This can be done by gradually forcing the child to awaken earlier even on the weekends. A counselor may refer the parents to a specialist in the disorders of sleep disturbance in children.

Nightmares. Nightmares are simply an example of underlying fear expressed during sleep. The child, when awakened, can frequently describe a terrible nightmare. Fears, anxiety, and sadness usually accompany the nightmare's description. Even though the child, when awake, recognizes that the nightmare was a dream, the fright the child experiences does not diminish.

The counselor needs to advise the parents to accept the child's fear as real and not to just dismiss it as a bad dream. The parent may need to spend some time in the child's room to calm the child and decrease his or her anxiety. Sharing a bed with the parents should not become habitual. The child who has recurrent nightmares and whose degree of fear is unusually severe needs further evaluation and possible treatment by a qualified child therapist. These severe and frequent nightmares often signal an underlying emotional disturbance.

Sleep terrors. While nightmares occurring during REM sleep actually are dreams, night terrors occur from partial awakening from deep non-REM sleep. The child may sit up and stare blankly or perhaps even get up and walk around in a confused state as if he or she were searching for something. At other times, the child may act frantic, panicked, and scared and may actually carry on a conversation with an adult who comes into the room. The conversations that occur, however, are not meaningful.

The name *night terrors* accurately describes the symptoms these children display, since they literally are in a terror and cannot seem to be calmed. When the child is fully awakened, he or she is calm and ready to go back to sleep and does not remember the episode of "terror."

Sleep terrors generally occur for only a few minutes but may last up to fifteen minutes or longer. The counselor can educate parents to the difference between sleep terrors and nightmares. The sleep terror should be allowed to run its course; parents should intervene only if necessary to protect the child from injury. Parents should realize that as the event ends, the child suddenly will become calm and will start stretching and yawning and will want to go back to sleep.

In general, the more serious disorders of early childhood are noticed first by the parent, but then frequently they require a work-up by a professional with specific expertise in the problem area. In treating serious childhood disorders, the counselor is frequently well utilized as an effective coordinator of the practical needs of the family, the instructional and supportive needs of the parents, and therapeutic needs of the child.

PART TWO

THE GRADE-SCHOOL CHILD

CHAPTER EIGHT

NEEDS OF THE GRADE-SCHOOL CHILD

IN GREAT DISTRESS, Abby visited a counselor about her daughter Jenny, a first grader. Abby believed Jenny was experiencing emotional problems. As a preschooler, Jenny's greatest delight had been to accompany her mother to the grocery store and on other Saturday errands, Abby told the counselor. At home, the girl liked to sit attentively beside her mom while she sewed, watching as Abby pored over her craft projects.

However, since Jenny had entered first grade, she seemed to be growing apart from her mother. On Saturdays, Jenny now preferred to play with friends rather than spend time with Abby.

The counselor assured Abby that Jenny's behavior was perfectly normal for children who are entering school and are approaching their seventh birthdays. At that age, children suddenly begin to enter the world at large. They will begin to cut the emotional apron strings, a process that in an emotionally healthy child will continue through adolescence.

During this period, there are at least four major areas in which children need success. These are (1) material, (2) mental, or cognitive, (3) relational, and (4) self-esteem.

PROVIDING MATERIAL NEEDS

Until age six, the parents have provided the child's material needs. But once the child reaches school age, he or she begins to feel the need to work toward earning, rather than being entitled to, some of the material things in life.

Obviously, parents still carry the major responsibility of meeting the child's material needs. But the child should have the opportunity to feel successful in earning an allowance, privileges, and "special treats" for responsibilities or chores.

In our materialistic culture, children have not always had to work for and earn things of material importance to them. This can have the unwanted psychological effect of encouraging the child to pass through the key, school-age developmental years and adopt, all too easily, a teen-age-consumer pattern of life.

Of course, Madison Avenue finds great advantage in pushing the child into this arena as soon as possible. The sooner the child begins consuming like an adult, the sooner he or she (or the parent who is pressured by the child) spends larger amounts of money.

But children are better off if they proceed slowly through these school-age years and develop an orderly pattern of working, earning, saving, and responsibly spending money for material items. Also, in this age bracket, children should increase their capacity to care for possessions responsibly. From being assigned to feed the dog to remembering to check the mail, grade-school children find this an ideal time to begin learning the merits of earning and caring for goods.

The need for children to carry a major load of home chores has all but disappeared in this culture. Grace W. Weinstein in *Children and Money* says, "Most of the tasks necessary for family survival in the past were tasks that could be shared with children, even young children. Each pair of hands was a pair of hands to be put to work as early as possible at tending goats, finding and chopping firewood, making soap and candles."[1] Although this need for children to help with home chores may have diminished, the benefits of it have, if anything, increased with our more modernized society.

Frances Cogle Lawrence, associate professor of home economics at Louisiana State University, studied 105 Southern families, looking at the various types of household tasks children performed. In a 1982 article, she reported that children spent the most time—about ten minutes a day—on activities involved with maintaining the home, yard, pets, cars, etc. Housecleaning was second, with nine minutes; food preparation was seven minutes; dishwashing, four minutes; and care of clothing and linens, one minute.[2]

Younger children do more chores and activities which center on themselves, such as making beds, picking up toys, and cleaning up their rooms, whereas grade-school children perform activities involving work for the family unit, such as yard work and caring for younger siblings.

Elliott Medrich of the Children's Time Study at the University of California, Berkeley, says, "Given the types of chores, it's probably not surprising that children we surveyed did not see their contribution as significant or important."[3] Chores sometimes appear to require little creativity or initiative and don't inspire much concern for others. Yet, given the potential benefits involved in household tasks, parents should try to motivate and encourage these young workers in any constructive way possible.

In a popular article entitled "Child Labor," Elin McCoy notes several mistakes parents make when motivating children to do household tasks. She says parents and children don't do enough chores together; working together requires cooperation and coordination of effort. Thus, it offers a chance for family members to learn to depend on each other to accomplish a task. They also can learn confidence through relying on fellow family members.

One family we know designated Thursday nights as "family clean-up night." It became a ritual that everyone actually looked forward to. After a home-delivered pizza, the four family members each did their assigned chores. (Even a preschooler can empty wastebaskets and help dust knickknacks and pictures.) The event removed the boredom from housecleaning and turned it into fun.

Sometimes, parents do not give their children enough interesting tasks or chores with any inherent value. Children who perceive household tasks as mere busy work will be bored easily. Parents should show children that, with a bit of creativity, even "boring" chores can be highly valuable—even enjoyable.

Parents sometimes are ambiguous about the performance standards they have set for housework. Children need to be able to look at what they have done and clearly see whether they have accomplished the assigned task according to standard. If they do not know whether they are doing a good job, it is hard for them to feel good or confident about it. Medrich, in the book alluded to earlier, points out the value of a written description of a "neat room."

Parents may need cautioning not to ask too much from their children lest the children resent their tasks. At best, childhood is a fleeting time; its joys and carefree aspects should be protected. However, the benefits of children taking responsibility and performing household tasks are documented overwhelmingly.

Cheryl, a young widowed mother with two children, wanted (and desperately needed), her daughters to help with the housework. But she didn't want to be overly critical of their rudimentary efforts. Developing a schedule in which she and her two children switched tasks each week ensured that Cheryl would perform all of the household tasks once every three weeks. Therefore, even if daughter Sally's job of scrubbing the toilets definitely left something to be desired, Cheryl didn't criticize because she knew she soon would have a chance to restore order.

As McCoy says, "It's true that most children's work today can't offer the richness and human rewards it could in the past, but the lessons—about sharing tasks, building family solidarity, and meeting challenges—still can be learned."[4]

ACQUIRING COGNITIVE GROWTH

The child's mind in these grade-school years is expansive, creative, and curious in nature. The child enjoys learning, whether at home, in the classroom, or on a playing field. This is a normal phenomenon and one to be encouraged. Therefore, parents must give a child in this age bracket the learning experiences and activities which challenge a child's mind to expand.

At the same time, however, parents should be sure these activities are not overly competitive nor communicated in a threatening or discouraging atmosphere. Parents must recognize individual differences in children if the child is to progress in an orderly fashion through these years.

One area in which parents sometimes subtly communicate harmful information is in sex-role stereotypes. The counselor should help parents overcome the time-worn practice of encouraging boys to be achievement-oriented and emotionally strong (and often nonexpressive emotionally) and encouraging girls to be appearance-oriented and "people-pleasing" in mentality. As counselors, we have all seen numerous men striving to gain self-worth from achievement and competition while shunning any emotional expression and living in total misunderstanding of their own deeper emotional needs. On the other hand, we have counseled women who were appearance-oriented, believing their worth came from pleasing others. Such women often are uneasy when trying to express themselves honestly or with appropriate assertiveness.

When Brent first came home from school wanting to sign up for a homemaking course, his father's response was, "But that's for girls!" His comment discouraged Brent, who was eager to take the course.

The father didn't realize that schools today have revamped the stereotypical homemaking curriculum of cooking and sewing to include topics like child care, baby-sitting, and financial management, topics that appeal to both sexes.

If the father had asked a few questions instead of reacting with a stereotype, he could have learned that more than half of the students in the class were male. Even the sewing component found the male students making colorful knee-length shorts that everyone really liked. And what young man doesn't need to learn to sew on buttons or repair a pants leg hem?

One way to discourage sexual stereotypes is to allow both boys and girls to demonstrate their emotional vulnerabilities and to learn that expressing honest emotional needs is a sign of neither weakness nor immaturity. Both parents need to be available emotionally, and children should be encouraged to develop their natural interests and abilities.

Being sensitive to the child's gifts and abilities not only encourages the child but makes the child aware that he or she is a special creation of God. The grade-school years represent an ideal time to reinforce the child's belief in his or her own ability to address a task, to understand the requirements for accomplishing a task, and to confidently carry out a plan of action.

Persistence is learned during this phase of a child's development. The learning-disabled child who loses heart and labels himself or herself a "loser" in this period is sad to see. Such children are eager to learn and intelligent, but they frequently can't perform what they have learned because of the neurologically based difficulty of expression. Children are expected to perform in keeping with the rigid standards of the classroom environment. Unless such children are helped by trained teachers and programs designed for their needs, they may haplessly fulfill their "dropout" self-prophecy later on.

BECOMING SUCCESSFUL IN RELATIONSHIPS

A child in the grade-school age bracket wants to experience success in relationships with peers, siblings, parents, and other significant adults. Children of this age can be easy and fun to work with since they so desire to win adult approval, are eager learners, and willingly seek to comply with expected norms.

Adults must provide good models of behavior in this age group for these children commonly form heroes and develop ideals of behavior. In developing worthy heroes, a child develops a sense of respect for others—especially adults—a crucial component of a whole and healthy personality. This sense of respect later translates to an ability to work with authority figures, to value proven traditions appropriately, and to pass a sense of heritage along to the next generation.

Parents are responsible for drawing out and refining the child's developing sense of respect and fairness toward others. James P. Comer, Maurice Falk Professor of Child Psychiatry at Yale University's Child Study Center, says, "The issue, again, is respect. Although sometimes hidden, youthful idealism and the desire for respect are there; it helps if parents call for respect in the spirit of fair play. Young people this age are very conscious of relationships with others."[5]

Comer notes that children can more readily conceptualize the principle of respecting others when they see parents demonstrating respect for one another, and also for children and for community standards as well. Children, he says, naturally apply the Golden Rule to situations in virtually every setting, especially in terms of relationships. If children cannot develop successful relationships in appropriate ways, then they will use inappropriate means (negative options) to achieve some satisfaction in relationships.

ESTABLISHING SELF-ESTEEM

In this stage of childhood, the young person is exposed to a barrage of new ideas, experiences, and social settings. So that this avalanche of experiences will not overwhelm the developing young mind, the child seeks to understand his or her environment. Ideally, the child draws deeply from his or her experiences with both parents and from the values and behavior norms taught at home.

This child needs to take what is learned at home and move it into the open marketplace of neighborhood peer relationships, the classroom, the church, and anywhere the child goes. The counselor will help not only the child but also the parents believe that the world "makes sense."

Children in this developmental stage commonly are buoyed with optimism and enthusiasm for tasks they face. However, theirs is not an impregnable fortress of optimism and enthusiasm. They are susceptible to stresses and changes which threaten to overwhelm their capacities to adapt. Even though it sounds simplistic, the antidote to stress-caused problems is for these children to progressively develop a sound self-concept.

It has been suggested that a child's emerging self-concept involves three stabilizing points.

Attitude 1—A Sense of Belonging. This involves the child understanding—through words, through actions, and through the parents' reflected priorities—that, "I am wanted" and "I am needed," versus feeling isolated and "in the way." The child picks this up in the parents' verbal communications, body language, and actions that convey a thankful attitude because the child is part of the family.

Attitude 2—A Sense of Worth. Worth pertains not only to the family's love for the child but also to the child's having an inherent value to the parents, later to peers and community, and ultimately to God. Statements such as "I have a purpose" or "I count for something" are the self-talk echoing inside the child's mind. A child who feels he or she is worth something to the parents and to God will in time want to be worth something to society, to the church, and to the world.

Attitude 3—A Sense of Confidence. Confidence is the antithesis of hopelessness. No parent wants to instill in a child a sense of arrogance and of total self-centeredness. But we rarely see overdeveloped self-confidence. More often, counselors see children with an underdeveloped self-confidence, children with shallow, impulsive, and destructive compensations for their lack of self-assurance.

One example is the class clown, who is loud, who gets in trouble, and who seems unable to appreciate others' feelings. Actually, this child may instead be insecure and frightened. Such children may seek to "scare off" their own apprehensions by seeming to have no needs, fears, or self-doubts.

Parents sometimes can create a crisis in self-image by praising or reinforcing for superficial characteristics. For example, this can occur when parents unduly emphasize appearance or performance. We all know that gold medals in the Olympics are awarded for the most developed physical skills, and not for character. Competition to some extent is healthy, but some parents seem to have an achievement-at-any cost mentality. This can significantly damage the young child's sense of self-esteem and defeat any lasting attempt at building a biblical value system.

Parents also can err if they emphasize status and prestige. Children watch what parents buy, where they live, what they drive, and what they do with their spare time. They continually observe whether parents place a high value on social position, status, or accolades from others. Children also notice if parents belittle or find fault in others in the neighborhood, at church, or in politics.

A parent who hears a child come home from school with comments like, "I hate Manny; he's an idiot," or "she is such a jerk" may be horrified at such strong terminology. But the parent should look at how he or she talks about others when the child is present. Often the child gossips or criticizes simply to model what he hears a parent say.

Children who see their parents emphasizing status and especially taking the opportunity to cut others down quickly will be damaged by this. This will lead them to develop self-concepts fueled in part by the need to protect and provide for oneself at any cost. This is an unfortunate self-image concept to be carried into adulthood and it certainly breeds a host of unbiblical response patterns later.

We have sought in this chapter to show that the grade-school child begins to be involved in an "extended family" experience in which the family—of which the child is now a part—is extending itself into the neighborhood, the church, the school, and to the larger world. In the teen-age years, the peer group and surrounding environment become even more potent factors in the young person's development and growth. Erik Erikson has described the grade-school age as a time of industry (the ability to confidently achieve) versus inferiority (the sense of being unable to keep up with the world around).[6] Therefore, children in grade-school years need to obtain more than grades, trophies, or status. They also must develop a consistent pattern of self-confidence and a healthy view of themselves in relation to personal needs and to an emerging walk with God.

CHAPTER NINE

OPTIONS OF THE GRADE-SCHOOL CHILD

FRED FREQUENTLY STARTED A PROJECT, such as painting the kitchen of his home, and then stopped before the task was halfway finished. Some emergency always seemed to prevent Fred from ever completing any task, so his home was filled with half-painted rooms, half-repaired screens, and weedy flower beds.

Was it any wonder, then, that Fred and his wife Imogene were called to a parent-teacher conference about their son Nate, who always seemed to dawdle over finishing his work in class? Fred had failed to model for Nate the importance of hanging in there and completing a task.

The child who is successful in the four areas described in

the previous chapter will show he or she is developing positively in at least the following four characteristics: (1) perseverance, (2) achievement, (3) worth and acceptance, and (4) belonging.

PERSEVERANCE

Perseverance is the ability to set aside immediate gains in order to work hard and achieve more rewarding, distant accomplishments. The parent should help the child persevere.

Trying hard and continuing to do a good job regardless of immediate results is a valuable quality indeed. In seeking ways to help a child—such as Nate—develop perseverance, the counselor might share the following four Rs with the child's parents:

Reward perseverance, not necessarily just achievement. Many times, children feel perseverance is only valuable if they achieve their ultimate goal. Parents can be caught up in this as well and can neglect to reward the child or praise the child for having persevered regardless of the outcome.

In the grade-school years, learning to persevere at a task may be more important than is the actual success of the outcome. Success may come later in life as the person acquires more skills, but perseverance is necessary to pursue any worthy objective.

Reduce the load. Some children have so many things to do that they can experience an "activity glut." One mother breathed a sigh of relief every Thursday because that was her child Jon's only free day—the only day of the week he could play with friends after school instead of leaving for some extracurricular activity. Jon was only a second grader, not a high-school senior like the activity level might indicate.

Although some children thrive on pursuing many interests, this excess of channels for them to follow sometimes leads to the frustration that they are never really good at any one task. Parents of grade-school-age children will want to avoid the circumstances in which their youngsters might feel they are jacks of all trades, and masters of none.

Reflect perseverance in the parental example.

Rescue not. Parents who care greatly for their children sometimes step in and help them finish tasks. Or they correct errors in their children's performance, or confront teachers if children seem overlooked. One mother telephoned her daughter's teacher any time she complained that she didn't get a part in a play or that her work wasn't picked for display. Occasionally, the beleaguered teacher gave in under pressure and made sure the child received recognition, earned or not. In the short run, this may have improved the child's grade, but it also sapped her sense of independence and responsibility. It is unwise for the parent to step in and meddle with the child's work effort and thereby interrupt the child's personal completion of the task. In general, a child persevering 100 percent on an assignment which results in a C grade is better than one persevering 70 percent and, with parental help, achieving an A.

Psychologists Julius and Zelda Segal write that "perseverance is not a trait you can bequeath to your child to use in life as needed. Sometimes the attitude must be learned the hard way, after difficult episodes of frustration, conflict and anger. But we can smooth that learning process and help our youngsters realize the delicious rewards that eventually belong to those who stay the distance even when the road is long."[1]

ACHIEVEMENT

Achievement pertains to that sense of tenacity and competitive verve which a child learns to expend in actually grasping a goal. Interestingly, those who normally push grade-school children hardest are the children themselves. One first grader cried hysterically after school one day when she failed to make her usual 100 on a spelling test. She was disappointed in herself for not measuring up to her own high standards.

Parents know that the pressure to succeed is part of life, and children need to learn to cope with it whether they like it or not. But it is wise for parents to communicate that winning is not everything. If Mom and Dad inherently are high achievers, or if the child overhears them bragging about the child's successes, he or she will pick up the message that winning is a high priority in the family.

Parents of fast-track children are told to "raise your sights a little lower," by David and Barbara Bjorklund, psychologists at Florida Atlantic University. They add: "These children often leave a structured and competitive school environment to partake in high-pressure after-school activities. Dancing, piano, tennis and karate lessons may fill children's afternoons. In most cases, these activities are competitive, with children striving to win trophies and honors."[2]

This places the child under a rather persistent strain of achievement-oriented thinking and high levels of self-driven expectation. However as Hilda Besner, a psychologist in Fort Lauderdale, Florida, points out, it also orients children to seeing other children as potential competitors and therefore as threats to their success. This can drive a wedge between the normal and healthy friendships that ideally form and blossom in the grade-school years.[3]

Parents who are relaxed about achievement and who communicate a calm and balanced attitude toward their children develop a healthy balance between the joy of participating and striving for first place. Dr. Besner also recommends that parents and children spend more time relaxing around one another and enjoying activities that aren't necessarily geared to produce anything.

WORTH AND ACCEPTANCE

School-age children who are meeting their needs will develop an ever-solidifying sense of self-worth and acceptance of their personhood. This will include their gifts, abilities, and limitations. Children naturally will seek options that make possible their developing sense of worth and acceptance. If positive options are not available, they invariably will seek negative ones. For example, the child with a learning problem (which may prevent experiencing worth and acceptance in the school setting) may seek attention by being the class clown, avoiding school work.

BELONGING

Although team sports are not for all children, most children in the grade-school years tend to take team sports rather naturally. During this stage, parents see emerging their children's sense of sportsmanship and the capacity to be a part of a team to pursue joint goals.

There are several advantages of team sports. Each child can learn that players on a team will have different jobs. At first, every child wants to be where the action is. But as children learn to play a team sport, they learn to play their position and carry out their assigned jobs. This opportunity to set aside immediate enjoyment and excitement for the sake of self-disciplined service of the team's overall good is a valuable lesson children can learn from team sports.

The child also learns how to share the "glory" of victory without hogging all the credit. Learning to take pride in the fact that "*we* won" versus "*I* won" instills in children the mutuality-of-effort concept.

By belonging to a team, the child learns self-sacrifice for the team's good. The child learns that at times one must actually give away an advantage.

A Little Leaguer in one family was asked to lay down a sacrifice bunt. He knew enough to realize that by doing so his batting average would shrink. At that point, he was competing with several other outfielders in the league for the best batting average. This kind of self-sacrifice at the coach's direction, for the good of the team, was a valuable lesson.

Team sports teach the child patience. Anyone who has ever played team sports has experienced sitting on the bench, feeling that he or she could contribute to the team effort, yet being asked by the coach to play only a supportive role. This helps children realize the importance of teamwork and patience.

Also, the child learns to lose without blaming others. David marveled the day his son Joey commented after losing a soccer game, "None of us played terrific, Dad," rather than his usual diatribe about the goalie's mistakes. Among grade-school players, a wide disparity of skill level likely exists. Because of developmental differences in this age group, some children play well relatively all the time, whereas other children often drop ground balls or miss the goal with their kicks. Learning how to share the glory of a victory is a valuable part of team sports, but so is learning to lose without criticizing other players who possibly are less skilled.

By playing team sports, the child also learns to practice in unison. The concept of practice, especially as a team, is usually a new one for the grade-school-ager. These children learn to work without immediate rewards, train to face a team that isn't even on the practice field, and participate with their teammates in that preparation. "Everybody wants to be somebody, nobody wants to grow," Goethe said. In the vernacular of grade-school team sports, that line translates: "Everybody wants to hit a home run; nobody wants to just knock practice balls." The child learns that practicing to be ready to win has every bit as much to do with success as does the actual effort during the game.

The child also learns perseverance and loyalty to the group by being a team member. Every grade-school coach experiences that mid-season "slump" when practice attendance begins to wane and team members begin thinking of other pursuits. Following through on commitments to the team and staying involved both for one's own sense of accomplishment and for loyalty to the team itself is a valuable outcome of team sport participation.

No matter how valuable team sports are, however, all children should not be forced into them. Nor should children who don't gravitate toward team sports be made to feel that they are somehow less than normal.

Parents sometimes push their children into team sports either prematurely or for the wrong reasons. "Families should not become involved in team sports because the parents want to, but they should become involved because the children want to," say David and Barbara Bjorklund. ". . . the parents' role should be a supportive one. Parents should remember during games that it's their children's show and that they are merely there as spectators."[4]

Children who join groups such as Boy Scouts or Girl Scouts or Indian Guides receive some of the same benefits as do those who take part in team sports. At this stage, children enjoy being part of a body of people pursuing a larger purpose for the common good. Children in these groups develop a strong sense of same-sex loyalty and unity which contributes to a positive self-concept. Youngsters will carry this self-concept with them into the peer-pressure years of adolescence.

POSITIVE OPTIONS

The child in the grade-school years has some twelve basic options to pursue.

1. *Learning delayed gratification, or learning how to work now and enjoy the benefits of that labor later.*

2. *Learning responsibility for meeting some of one's own needs, especially material and friendship needs.*

3. *Learning the "investment principle" of working to achieve long-term goals.* This is somewhat different than delayed gratification. This option teaches the child that preparing for a task sometimes teaches the greatest lessons and skills.

Marty studied hard and long for a history competition involving students across the state. His teacher knew that the competition's size made it unlikely that any students from Marty's school would win first place, but she tried to make the preparation sessions fun and valuable for the students. Although Marty didn't take top prize, the history review helped him learn important facts which were never covered in class. In this case, the preparation was more important than the actual outcome.

4. *Learning that sibling rivalry (or rivalry among peers in the neighborhood) can help children resolve conflicts in a positive fashion.*

5. *Learning a proper view of competition.* Learning to balance the desire to win with the philosophy of playing the game for enjoyment. A wise soccer coach called parents of his team members after every game to check on each team member. The coach told the parents, "I'm not concerned with whether we won last Saturday. I'm concerned with whether your child is really having fun."

6. *Learning to develop healthy relationships between peers (primarily other children of the same sex).*

7. *Learning to develop interests in hobbies, sports, creativity, and group activities.* These often begin with family ties but extend outside the family boundaries as the grade-school child becomes more involved in the ebb and flow of social interactions.

8. *Learning scholastic achievement.* Learning how to follow through on school assignments is an important option, as is realizing the value of achievement in a school situation.

9. *Learning an increasingly broad view of their place in the world.* This includes sharing, cooperation, and a sense of common loyalty among people.

10. *Learning an appropriate curiosity about physical and sexual identity.* Developing a sense of self-identity and building this up to a level of strength will enable most children to sustain the inevitable challenges of the adolescent turmoil.

11. *Learning to accept rules and conditions that appropriate adults place on the school-age child.* The child learns to live in peace within reasonable limits, and comes to trust authority figures and believe in the overall goodness of societal norms.

12. *Learning an overall concept of fairness and justice.* The grade-school child is especially sensitive to issues of fairness and justice. Fair play, honesty, loyalty, and a sense of camaraderie all help the child balance the intensely self-directed issues of the first six years of life with the other-directed issues of the grade-school years.

NEGATIVE OPTIONS

Grade-school children also have negative options for meeting some of their needs. Parents must realize their children are not being simply bad for no reason. Instead, they are willfully choosing a negative option—such as direct disobedience—which both parent and child fully understand.

However, sometimes neither parents nor children understand the negative options children are choosing. The counselor may need to sift through many apparently inexplicable and disconnected behaviors in trying to find some organizing themes. As we suggested twelve positive options the school-age child may choose, we now turn to twelve negative options among which this child may choose to meet his or her needs.

1. *Refusing to invest in normal-range, achievement-oriented activities.* This can involve failing to be prepared for school and social tasks, refusing to attend school, or withdrawing from normal and healthy competitive activities with other children in the neighborhood.

2. *Attempting to be overly perfectionistic or irresponsible.* A child might shirk responsibilities and become less willing to comply with parents' expectations. Or, he or she may attempt the reverse—becoming hyperresponsible, trying to control the lives of those around him or her who might seem in distress. This might push the child beyond his or her endurance level.

3. *Demanding immediate gratification.* If parents have used material gratification to compensate for emotional or personal struggles, then a child can start demanding more and more material goods as a way of meeting personal needs. The reasons why parents overgratify a child were discussed in chapter 7.

4. *Experiencing inappropriate or destructive sibling rivalry.* Manny, a ten-year-old, began picking incessantly on his five-year-old sister, teasing her to the point of tears, deliberately tripping her when she walked past him, pushing her out of chairs at the dinner table. All of this occurred about the time he was moved to a new school, where a "winning-is-everything" philosophy reigned. Although Manny was a good student, in this new setting he felt his worth was measured only by straight-A report cards and advanced placement programs. In therapy, a counselor helped the parents see how Manny's decreased sense of self-esteem contributed to problems at home, especially those involving his younger sister. With the therapist's help, the parents doubled their efforts to boost Manny's self-esteem and help him cope with the school transition.

5. *Developing an improper view of competition.* This involves an effort to win at any cost or to participate in sports with a "me-first" attitude. Children may receive short-term gains as they push ahead of their peers at any cost, but later, the backlash of lost relationships and the ever-present fear of failure take their toll on children's emotional health.

6. *Displaying scholastic misachievement or failing in school in an attempt to humiliate the parents or the child.* When Lisa's dad took a new job requiring him to travel out of town on frequent business trips, her grades suddenly took a pronounced tumble without any solid academic reason for the plunge. A counselor helped Lisa's parents see that Lisa felt overlooked and left out as a result of her dad's frequent absences. To ensure she got her dad's attention, Lisa deliberately slacked off in school.

7. *Developing a self-protective view of the world.* Seeing others in a skeptical light, the child withdraws from emotional involvement with them. Children use this option as a way to protect themselves from environmental stresses.

8. *Suffering from too much stress.* Counselors and parents can help understand a child's reactions if they know to what

degree life events impact the child. Figure 9–1 shows clusters of events that place a child under various levels of stress. Although this chart is not scientifically quantified, it is based on our observations in clinical practice. We have seen that these events generally weigh on the child with either a super amount of stress, a very high amount of stress, a high amount of stress, or a moderate amount.

Children who have lost a parent or both parents by death are said to be under extreme stress. They are thought to be in the Very High Stress category for a year following the loss, during which time they are at risk for severe health impairment or emotional upset.

Children with two or three events in the Very High Stress category (column 1) have an increased chance of being emotionally impaired. Those with two or three of the events from column 2 are predisposed to emotional difficulty. If just a few more causes of stress entered their lives, they would also be in the high-risk group—susceptible to severe sickness or emotional problems.

No hard-and-fast rule can tell the counselor how many events must occur to stress a child's life significantly. However, if several of these events occur in a cluster—especially if they are weighted toward the very high and high stress columns—the counselor should be aware that he or she must intervene and assist the child and the parents.

9. *Beginning to defy and disobey legitimate authority.* Primarily the parents are the child's target; but also the school, church, or community authorities may become the object of his or her resistance.

10. *Developing a poor concept of justice and fairness and seeing life as patently unfair.* This reflects a child who has become disillusioned and discouraged with the prospects of meeting his or her needs in what is perceived as an inequitable system.

11. *Experiencing inappropriate feelings regarding physical and sexual identity.* This includes confused sexual identity and early sexual acting out, and also involves deep-seated misgivings about the child's own physical attributes.

12. *Stagnating of the child's personality because of parental overshadowing or overcontrol.* Parents who want to force their

Very High Stress	High Stress	Moderate Stress
1. The parents divorce or separate.	1. The child changes to a new school (or has a new teacher). This includes a first grader just beginning school.	1. The family moves to a new house or neighborhood (not involving a change in schools).
2. A close family member has a major health change. This includes the mother's becoming pregnant.	2. Parents have significant fights between themselves or have fights of intensity with the child's siblings or with in-laws. This especially applies if the child is caught in the middle.	2. The child has a change in responsibility at home.
3. The child has a major school problem—for example, a suspension or failing grade.	3. A parent abuses drugs or alcohol.	3. The child feuds with children in the neighborhood or has a change in friends.
4. A sibling is born or dies.	4. The child is threatened or has major fights at school, or there are major disturbances and conflicts between the child and a fellow sibling.	4. The child has a decrease in grades or has teacher-compatibility problems (including minor to moderate discipline problems at school).
5. A parent loses his or her job, adversely affecting the finances and stability of the home.	5. The child loses a pet or has an important personal possession stolen.	5. One or both parents has a work schedule change.

6. Mother begins working outside the home for the first time.	6. An older sibling leaves home.	6. The child achieves significant personal success for which he or she is recognized.
7. The child has a major health problem. This is especially stressful if hospitalization is required.	7. The child begins a new extracurricular activity or changes extracurricular activities. For example, a child who begins to play soccer for the first time or who stops taking piano and tries out for gymnastics.	7. The child attends summer camp or takes a long vacation with the family.
	8. The child has a religious conversion—for example, a child becomes a born-again Christian.	8. The child has some event that disrupts the usual schedule of daily activities, especially if sleeping and eating habits or routines have been changed.
		9. The extended family has strife. For example, the family experiences problems with cousins, or difficulties with grandparents.

Figure 9–1
Childhood Stress Checklist

child into a preconceived mold often use the grade-school years to pursue this objective. For example, the father who always dreamed of being a major league baseball player might pressure his son to excel in baseball during these middle years of childhood. Or, the mother who always wanted to become a professional dancer may choose these years to unduly pressure her daughter to participate in the city's youth ballet.

The child responds either by attempting to comply with this parental pressure or by rebelling wholeheartedly against any parental encroachments into his or her world. Choosing either of these negative options will impair the child's personal development.

CHAPTER TEN

WAYS FOR CHANGE WITH THE GRADE-SCHOOL CHILD

EVER SINCE THEIR FIRST CHILD WAS A TODDLER, the Darby family made bedtime prayers a priority. Both parents said individual prayers with each child. As they prayed, the mother and dad frequently thanked God for giving them Michael and Marcy to be part of the family.

Parents are sometimes surprised to learn what a great effect voicing their thankfulness for their youngsters in the children's presence has in making children feel loved and accepted.

If parents communicate love and acceptance through prayers and other ways, they find that children more readily accept limits and consequences because these actions do not harm their sense of self-worth. Setting limits and consequences is a vital way for change in helping grade-school children select positive options mentioned in the previous chapter rather than the negative ones. This chapter deals with ways for change that will help the child choose positive courses of action.

RELATIONSHIPS

Healthy relationships are a major key in helping children grow and change. Growing and changing begins in the parent-child relationship. Parents must be committed to truly loving their children, that is, committed to doing whatever is in the best interest of their children. That kind of love often is not much fun. Taking a stand as a parent often means disagreement with the child, but it always seeks the best interest of the child. That kind of love is not self-serving to the parents. Remember, children don't exist to meet the needs of adults.

Parents must be committed to modeling for their children that problems are best solved in relationships. Children will learn problem-solving skills in a family where problems are discussed and solutions are employed after discussion. Children find it hard to grow and change when in the family problems are avoided, or the solution is blaming or escaping or simply punishing.

Children best grow and change when they feel an "affiliation" with the parents. In other words, the children sense the parents have empathy with their children and are willing to pursue common feelings and activities. There is no substitute for time spent by parents with their children. *Quality* time is only possible when there is sufficient *quantity* of time spent between parents and children.

It is also important that parents encourage relationships between their school-age children and healthy other adults such as teachers, coaches, or church workers. These relationships are essential to the child's growth and development and problem-solving skills.

Parents need to also encourage healthy peer relationships in the grade-school-aged child. These peer relationships help the child develop an understanding of his or her own identity and his or her own strengths and weaknesses while developing healthy problem-solving skills. Grade-school children will naturally seek relationships with same-sex peers.

Parents can also enhance a child's growth by encouraging a relationship with God. As this age child loses interest in fantasy and fairy tales, it is crucial he or she develop a relationship with a loving God who is available to aid in day-to-day living.

GOALS

Goals are important in helping the grade-school child grow and change. Children this age are quite prone to striving for success and achievement; they do this to win approval. Therefore, helping a child set realistic academic, athletic, spiritual, and social goals is quite important. The goals must be concrete enough to understand, realistic enough to ensure a reasonable chance of success, and high enough to require some "stretching" effort. Goals are best set with the interaction of the child and an adult. Achieving a goal needs to be appropriately reinforced. Approval by another person—especially an adult—is a powerful reinforcer. Care must be taken, however, for that adult to be supportive if a goal is not met. Failure to meet a goal should never affect a relationship's strength.

Often, parents help children set goals for the child that are actually a measure of the parents' need for their own achievement and acceptance. This eventually creates anger and rebellion in the child. Children do not exist to meet the achievement needs of parents. Counselors will want to assist parents in uncovering and resolving such problems.

The principle that approval can be conditional, but acceptance must never be, is one that parents will want to understand and practice.

EXPECTATIONS

Various parental expectations are a natural part of the child-rearing process. Power struggles serve only to alienate and humiliate. The counselor should help the parent identify and avoid potential power struggles.

Parents should make their expectations of the child clear and consistent; they should explain, not justify. Justifying can give the child the impression that the parent is embarrassed or ashamed to have appropriate expectations for the child. It is better to say simply, "I'm removing your privilege of playing

135

with friends Tuesday because you failed to come inside when I called" rather than going through a long explanation about "this hurts me more than it does you" or "when I was your age, I always came when my parents called me."

It is more important for parents to be consistent in their expectations than it is to use an "ultimate consequence." For example, parents daily should insist that their child be home for dinner at a certain time. They should impose consequences any time the child misses. This is better than allowing the child to miss the appointed hour every night for a week without consequence, only to enact some ultimate consequence, such as no TV for a month, for the past violations.

RESPONSIBILITIES

Responsibilities are a good way for children to learn healthy and workable options to meet their needs. As we have discussed earlier, chores that take into account children's age and natural abilities are excellent ways for them to become responsible and learn the satisfaction of accomplishing tasks. The counselor can help parents develop a natural flow of responsibility. With greater age come greater responsibilities, with their accompanying levels of greater privilege.

The responsibility to act should be commensurate with the child's level of emotional and intellectual maturity. For example, a child should be left with baby-sitting responsibilities only when he or she demonstrates enough maturity to handle emergency situations that arise on such occasions.

Allowances are a good idea, especially when these are tied to principles of good money management, savings, and tithing. The child will develop self-confidence in not only handling responsibilities but also in the increased privileges and money management that accompany these responsibilities.

LIMITS AND CONSEQUENCES

In using limits and consequences, the counselor and parent must make sure they do not inadvertently reinforce negative behavior. The child, for example, who knows the only real attention he or she can get is negative attention ironically will seek to keep a level of discord and disharmony brewing with the parents. The child will do this to be sure the parents are staying involved and paying attention.

Corporal punishment, or spankings, still play a role in disciplining the grade-school-age child, although spankings should become less and less frequent and should be reserved for situations where the other consequences of a given action prove ineffective for change.

All limits and consequences work well only when they are enforced against a backdrop of acceptance and love that is readily communicated by the parents to the child. This communication should not be verbal only; there also should be the demonstration of love by the amount of time parents spend with the child. Parents also can show their acceptance by communicating interest in the child's activities and by the sense of thankfulness to the Lord mentioned at the beginning of this chapter. Thanking the Lord for the child during nightly prayers should not be overdone, lest the child sense that Mom and Dad are merely paying lip service to the idea.

Another important aspect of limits and consequences concerns restitution. Children at this age should make restitution for wrongs committed. An older brother who uses one of his little brother's new model racing cars without permission and breaks it should do more than just apologize. Parents should require the older brother to use some of his allowance to help replace the car.

THE SPIRITUAL TRAINING OF THE CHILD

The school-age child's spiritual training can be approached by looking closely at seven key words: understanding, appreciation, submission, development, clarification, learning, and balancing.

Understanding represents the child's need to grow in comprehending his or her significance to God and how obeying God directly parallels obedience to the parents in the formative years of life. Children who learn to obey their parents crisply and with a good attitude will find it is easier to bring their behavior into line with the principles of God's Word than do children who haven't learned this.

Appreciation involves the child's learning to understand that God has both love and justice in His nature. The child then will have a basis for a deep appreciation of God's love when he or she pleads for mercy because of personal wrongdoings.

Submission means that the child has learned to appropriately submit to reasonable authority. This trait also helps the child develop a respect for God's chain of command.

Development has to do with the child's acquiring a habit of honesty and dependability. These are a major foundation from which a child's psychological maturity progresses. The child who can be honest in a variety of situations and dependable in carrying out agreements he or she has made is a child well on the way to mature character formation.

Clarification is the child's ability to clarify what sin really is. The biblical definition of sin as separation from God, and sin's consequences, are great concerns to the school-age child. Grade-school children, at times, tend to overgeneralize and to see things in black and white. Children may easily lump actions into categories of "black," yet they will not recognize more subtle areas, such as honesty or unkindness to friends, as sin and in need of change.

Learning, here, means the child's gaining an understanding of the value of the family and learning the high premium God places on faithfulness between marital partners. By the time children are in the grade-school years, they have seen countless TV shows and movies about people whose marriages have dissolved under the pressure of incompatibility and lack of commitment. This has also happened to the parents of some of their friends. Children benefit greatly from seeing their parents demonstrate the biblical marital guidelines. This does not mean that the parents have perfect marriages, any more than parents are required to be perfect Christians in order for their children to model their lives after them. Yet, seeing their parents in a committed marriage relationship gives children a significant portion of their "believability" about the Christian life.

Balancing means that the child develops healthy work habits but also clearly appreciates the relative insignificance of material things. It is hard for parents, even with a counselor's aid, to help the child see that material goods do not represent the substance of a happy life. This is especially hard in a culture where working, earning money, and gaining and spending material wealth are so highly valued and so universally reinforced. Here the grade-school child probably learns as much by observation as by instruction. A father whose sense of priority leads him to devote too much time to earning money may as well have placed wax in his children's ears. They won't hear when he speaks about the futility of materialism and the dangers of pursuing wealth.

Parents of grade-school-age children have two major responsibilities: training and engaging. In training the child, the parent is responsible for orchestrating "how-to" experiences. These offer a tremendous amount of practical information which in many ways forms the basis for the child's future learning. The engaging process requires the parents to act as "brokers," to be sure the child is engaging properly in a variety of experiences. These experiences vary from parent-child interactions in the deepest moments of communication to something as simple as assuring that the child follows through on attending a birthday party after accepting an invitation.

Children during the middle years need many types of encounters and experiences, and they tend to be unbalanced in the way they select their own encounters. Much as a young child going down a cafeteria line may choose foods that look appealing but do not provide a balanced diet, so will the grade-school child need supervision to pick the most productive kinds of experiences.

Children in this age should form same-sex friendships, crystallize a sense of fair play, develop a belief in society's rules, and formulate an understanding for the existence of right and wrong.

During these years, the child develops an appreciation for the omnipotence and relevance of the Creator. The counselor who intervenes with a grade-school-age child, knowing that these are very impressionable years, will make every effort to make a positive impression. It will likely be a lasting one.

CHAPTER ELEVEN

ANGER AND SIBLING RIVALRY

SOME SITUATIONS THAT DEVELOP IN CHILD-REARING do not belong in any one particular category. Yet they are dilemmas that many parents recognize and for which they covet answers. In this and the following six chapters, we will examine some special situations that often tax parental skills. A counselor who understands the dynamics in some of these special areas can be valuable to parents who need help.

THE ANGRY CHILD

Virtually all children experience episodes of anger. Julius Segal, psychologist and author of the book, *Winning Life's Toughest Battles*, says that "all kids explode in anger at some time or another. It's important for parents to realize children encounter as many disappointments and frustrations as do adults, and they need parents to acknowledge and accept their feelings."[1]

Dr. Segal points out that accumulated research and current clinical information proposes that children need to learn at least three major lessons in order to deal effectively with anger. First, he says, the child should realize that anger is a normal emotion and not something that needs to be avoided. Unfortunately, sometimes children assume that only happy, compliant, and contented emotional expressions reflect a "good" child. This is a devastating message since the young child has a limited repertoire of emotional responses. Anger is one of the first and foremost means for honest interaction with one's environment.

The child who is pressured to become overly good or ingratiating can, in fact, develop a strong sense of repressed hostility which, in adults, is one of the most common factors in depression. Chronically repressed anger in the young child also may cause psychosomatic illness—asthma, allergies, stomach indigestion problems, abdominal cramps—and it may also cause difficulty in school work and peer relationships.

Allowing the child to understand that anger is a necessary and God-given emotion is vital to the child's healthy emotional development. Ephesians 4:26 echoes this, saying "Be angry, and yet do not sin." Feeling angry is one thing, but expressing that anger in negative means is another.

Second, the child should learn healthy ways to express anger. Having angry feelings is not carte blanche approval for violent acts or hostile behaviors. It is now well understood in psychological circles that allowing a child to express angry and hostile emotions in an unrestrained way does not protect the child against developing neuroses later.

Social psychologist Carol Tavris, author of *Anger: The Misunderstood Emotion,* says complete emotional liberty can be psychologically unhealthy for the child. Granting such liberty cannot be substantiated by research, she says; and it is less likely to produce emotional health in the child than emotional tyranny.[2]

Simply allowing a child to go kicking, hitting, or breaking

things does not teach a child to manage anger. It instead conveys the message that raw anger can be ventilated in any situation. It may, in fact, foster inappropriate aggression.

Third, says Segal, the child should realize that anger is not intended to become a frequently used coping mechanism. Rather, anger is a means of dealing with difficult situations where significant and honest emotional frustration or injury exists.

We tell parents that the four "stokers" which tend to germinate anger in the young child are:

- Loss of self-esteem
- Discouragement or disappointment
- Humiliation or embarrassment
- Feelings of being treated unjustly or insensitively

Parents should teach the child to develop alternate responses rather than follow a persistent pattern of angry expression. The Scriptures teach that a wise individual learns to avoid wrath and turn anger away (see Proverbs 15:1; Ephesians 4:26). It is probably no coincidence that the same word *mad* is used in the English vernacular for both insanity and anger.

Children who regularly blow up in anger to negotiate routine situations are known as bullies. The problems of bullies and the adverse effect they have on personal psychological development—theirs as well as that of other children—need to be examined.

It appears that no one truly is born to be a bully; bullying seems to be a learned behavior. Bullies are usually boys, often older than their victims; they tend to be at least of average intelligence but do relatively poorly in school. They have few really close friends. As a child learns to master situations by using hostile, bullying behavior, positive reinforcement occurs. Later, other socially appropriate skills—such as developing good friendships or manifesting good school performance—tend to deteriorate as the bullying behavior becomes the child's major coping mechanism.

Studies by Leonard D. Eron and colleagues at the University

of Illinois in Chicago also reflect a significant level of criminal conduct when bullies reach the adult years. Children who were bullies in the early grade-school years were more likely to have dropped out of school by age sixteen than their classmates. In their early thirties, they were more likely to be working in low-status jobs and to be involved in dysfunctional relationships, such as being abusive husbands or fathers, than were others of their contemporaries.

Females who were bullies did not seem to have quite the same adverse pattern of future life experience, although they tended to be parents who were harsh and punitive with their children, according to Eron's study.

Patterson, De Baryshe, and Ramsey have noted that coercive behaviors in the child tend to produce two reactions from the social environment; one is rejection by the normal peer group, and the other is academic failure.[3] It is well accepted that the progression of dysfunctional behavior into antisocial conduct follows something of a continuum. A depiction of this continuum can be made as seen in Figure 11–1.

Perhaps the saddest discovery of all is that adults who as children had been bullies turned out to have children who were bullies, too. This is possibly because 30 to 40 percent of the variance in antisocial behavior is accounted for by parenting practices and family interaction.[4] On the optimistic side, victims seemed not to experience the long-term adverse consequences associated with bullies.

Children whose overprotective parents have taught them, either directly or indirectly, that assertiveness and "sticking up for oneself" are unseemly behaviors risk ill treatment by bullies. However, youngsters who display an attitude of "I won't be walked on" and seem willing to stand up for their rights are less frequent targets for bullies.

We use a simple acrostic—K.I.S.S.—to help parents or adult caregivers to respond to the angry child.

K means allowing the child to *know* angry feelings without insisting that the child suppress or deny them. Parents should model the appropriate side of anger, the ability to handle anger without it dominating relationships.

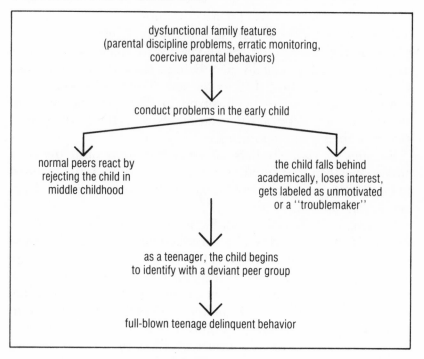

dysfunctional family features
(parental discipline problems, erratic monitoring,
coercive parental behaviors)

conduct problems in the early child

normal peers react by
rejecting the child in
middle childhood

the child falls behind
academically, loses interest,
gets labeled as unmotivated
or a ''troublemaker''

as a teenager, the child begins
to identify with a deviant peer group

full-blown teenage delinquent behavior

Figure 11–1

Allowing the child to see anger in the home in an appropriately managed fashion without the explosions that destroy relationships or home stability is important for the child.

One mother trained herself to talk slowly and quietly when she became angry. Instead of raising her voice, she found that lowering it and choosing her words extremely carefully helped her keep a lid on her anger and stay in control when feelings inside had reached a boiling point.

Parents should show affection, demonstrating that anger does not preclude intimacy. They should still try to give their youngster the usual goodnight hug and kiss even if anger has boiled up a few hours earlier. The "love-the-doer-but-hate-the-deed" maxim applies here once more. Parents should also explain situations. Sometimes children become angry when they don't understand what they perceive as unfairness or insensitivity in a parental decision. Jenny, seven, flared in anger when her mother insisted that she go with her on some errands while allowing Jenny's brother Adam, thirteen, to stay behind and play outdoors with friends. In saying that Adam was older and more able to take care of himself, the mother failed to explain that she planned to allow Jenny to play with her own friends as soon as the errands were finished, in an hour or so. To Jenny, the decision seemed patently unfair and final; the mother's explanation might have prevented Jenny's angry scene.

The *I* in the acrostic means that children can *instruct* themselves during angry times to "stay cool" and to think through the response they will make. Counting to ten when one is angry is not a bad message to convey to children. This especially helps when combined with phrases by which children can build their own self-esteem and decrease the need through positive self-talk to act out aggressively.

Solid Bible verses—for example, Proverbs 15:1, 18—about the wisdom of restraint and the use of kindness to solve situations help here. Building children's self-esteem and teaching them to express themselves verbally, in a more articulate way, are helpful.

Teaching children not only to instruct themselves cognitively but to develop a more adequate repertoire of verbal responses to others is important here. For example, rather than initiating a physical fight when a bully tries to take the child's bike, the child may learn to say, "I don't want you to ride my bicycle. I don't feel like sharing it right now. Maybe later."

This may sound a bit idealistic, but as children learn to deal with angry behavior, they can learn alternative phrases that deescalate situations rather than instigate altercations.

Also, teaching the child and parents to intentionally ignore inappropriate or inflammatory behavior is wise. Of course, certain situations cannot be ignored; but unnecessary altercations often arise when the child focuses on minor hassles or conflagrations.

Learning to ease tension with humor can be helpful, as many adults know. Some first-grade students felt hurt when a group of older pupils repeatedly called them "airheads." Their wise teacher told the younger group not to respond in anger and instead reply to the older students' taunts by saying, "Whoosh. I feel a draft!" fanning at their heads in an exaggerated, playful fashion.

"If the older students don't see they can make you angry, they'll decide to find something else to do," the teacher told her youngsters. And her plan soon worked.

Sometimes using delayed promises or rewards can help, too, in getting the child to step back from aggressiveness and to negotiate a more appropriate solution to a situation.

The first S in the K.I.S.S. acrostic is *setting limits*. The parent needs to set firm limits to prevent injury or inordinate hostile expressions. Physical restraint may be necessary, such as holding the child or removing the child from the scene to prevent injury. Giving the child the clear message of "no!" and backing that up with phrases showing the child that certain behaviors will not be permitted under any circumstance gives the child a sense of security. It also makes the parent seem believable to the child.

The second S stands for *shunting the anger*. The child should find ways to rechannel angry feelings that are "left over" after a situation has peaked. This also may help deescalate those angry feelings as well. Such activities as sports, exercise, music, or games are excellent ways to deescalate anger and redirect the child. One family always knew when a son's anger was deescalating because he went outside to bounce a basketball vigorously for a time. At other times, he rode his bike around the block to "cool off."

SIBLING RIVALRY AND COMPETITION

Probably no childhood experience frustrates parents more than does the problem of sibling rivalry. The constant arguing, bickering, and even fighting among their offspring frequently frustrates parents to the point of anger and rash threats.

Parents must remember that sibling rivalry is, indeed, a normal and essential part of each child's growing up. Through these conflicts children can begin to draw boundaries around their own identity, identify their strengths and weaknesses, and see the necessity of developing interpersonal skills.

Sibling rivalry injures children when no positive or fun times occur, or when one child inflicts severe physical or emotional injury upon another. In spite of parents' fears, this injurious rivalry is relatively rare. When increasing sibling rivalry occurs, it generally is not a problem with the children but with the parents.

One or more of three conditions usually is the cause of increased intensity in sibling rivalry.

1. *One or both parents consistently favors one child over the other(s).* Certainly some children, because of their temperaments and their consistent day-to-day behavior, are more likable than others. However, when a parent consistently begins to favor one child over another, rivalry between the children will become more frequent and more intense.

A fellow counselor worked with a woman in her seventies who harbored great disdain for her older sister and, in fact, rejoiced openly when she received word that the sister had died. The root of this lifelong rivalry was a mother who obviously and unabashedly had favored the older sister. The counselee had spent her life harboring a grudge against the sister because of the mother's partiality.

If the parents insist on yielding to the age-old battle cry of children, "it's not fair," sibling rivalry is bound to increase. The family system cannot exist solely on the concept of fairness. If fairness is the family's main goal, then older children cannot really receive extra privileges, and the child needing special help in one area or another cannot receive that help because "it's not fair."

In a previous example, Jenny, seven, cried "unfair" when her mother allowed Jenny's thirteen-year-old brother, Adam, to remain behind with friends while insisting that Jenny run errands with her. Her mother explained that Adam received extra privileges of being able to stay behind and regulate his own activities for the next hour because he was older and could take care of himself within certain parameters. But "fairness" was a concept that didn't especially apply in this case. Adam's age was the dominating factor in the mother's decision.

Fairness is based on moment-to-moment criteria, and on that moment-to-moment criteria, the child can't receive any special treatment. The issue really is not fairness, but justice involving what is in the best interest of each child, not only at present but also in the long run.

2. *Parents' marital difficulty.* Children are accurate barometers of the their parents' marriage. When increased conflict occurs between parents, sibling rivalry will usually increase. The children may well imagine, or hope, that if the parents have to stop a sibling wrestling match they will cease their own squabbling.

Carol and Jim were amazed to see how their frequent feuds affected their children's dispositions. When Carol and Jim were loving and thoughtful to each other, their two children seemed to have less conflict and competition and seemed to enjoy each other's company. But when the parents' cross words and discord increased, their son's and daughter's conflicts worsened. It is, indeed, true that children adopt the conflict-resolution skills modeled by their parents. It is also true that children are quite anxious when their parents are arguing and fighting. This anxiety leads to conflict with siblings not only as a means of venting their own anxieties but also frequently as a means of diverting the attention of the arguing, discordant parents toward the arguing, fighting children. In some way the children may prefer to have parents angry at them rather than see their parents angry at each other.

3. *Excessive involvement of a parent outside the home.* In our culture, one parent, particularly the father, is frequently too busy and wrapped up in the job and career. When this happens, sibling rivalry can serve as a warning signal; it is a cry for the absent parent to return home to attend to the family.

When a counselor helps parents deal with rivalry between children, one rule stands out: Parents should avoid mediating in sibling rivalry. If parents spend their energy trying to mediate this dispute, they will continually find themselves involved in the actual rivalry; and it will increase. Parents must remember that one of a child's purposes in sibling rivalry is to gain the parent as an ally against the other child. If the parents spend a great deal of energy trying to mediate sibling rivalry, they will eventually reinforce one child or the other; and the process will likely continue.

As a rule, parents should require their children to resolve the conflict. One warning for the argument and fighting to cease should be sufficient. If the children persist in their "war," then the parents must separate them. This sends the message that the parents will not be a part of the fighting and that siblings must resolve the issues themselves.

Counselors may aid parents by telling them that, despite all appropriate intervention, sibling rivalry likely will continue well into the children's teen-age years. Louis and Robert are brothers in their forties. Because they are good friends today, they now laugh about their constant battles as boys. But to their parents, the battles seemed unending until they were out of high school and on their own, when the bickering suddenly stopped.

Once children reach school age, competition becomes an important part of their lives. Although similar to sibling rivalry, competition plays a positive role in children's growth and development. While it is an important part of childhood, competition frequently is overemphasized to the child's detriment. Unhealthy competition between children is too often based on some unmet needs of the parents or other adults who are associated with these children.

Healthy competition needs at least two guidelines: (a) Situations involving competition among school-age children are either directly or indirectly supervised by healthy adults. The adults need not always be present, but at least they are available to resolve conflicts and to make sure competition does not get out of hand. (b) Healthy competition implies that every child in some arena of endeavor has the opportunity to win and lose. Competition is not healthy if a child never can win or lose.

Anger, conflict with peers, sibling rivalry, and competition are, indeed, part of every child's life. While they are often irritating to deal with they are opportunities for growth. The child who successfully learns to cope with these issues is well on the way to growing up and avoiding the pitfalls of depression and anxiety disorders described in the following chapter.

CHAPTER TWELVE

CHILDHOOD DEPRESSION AND THE FEARFUL, ANXIOUS CHILD

TWO OTHER SPECIAL PROBLEM AREAS that can occur during the school-age years are childhood depression and undue fear and anxiety. These two problems are discussed in this chapter.

CHILDHOOD DEPRESSION

In the past, experts doubted that children's personality structure was highly enough developed to manifest the classic signs of depression. However, within the last twenty years, research has shown that children do become depressed. Depression in childhood, while bearing some likeness to adulthood depression, is an entity unto itself.

Many authors have debated whether children demonstrate

actual depressed symptoms similar to those of adults—sadness, crying, suicidal thoughts—or whether most children develop depression equivalents, which include temper tantrums, fighting, aggressive behavior, irritability, and explosiveness. In the final synthesis, it seems that childhood depression has its own traits and symptoms. It is a true clinical phenomenon demanding accurate diagnosis and aggressive treatment.[1] The prognosis for the child whose depression is untreated is not good.

Various self-rating scales and parent-rating scales are available to help confirm a depression diagnosis in children. The diagnostic criteria for childhood depression include the following:

1. Dysphoric (sad) mood or loss of interest or pleasure in all, or almost all, activities and pastimes. For children under six, one may infer a child has a dysphoric mood if the child wears a persistently sad facial expression.
2. Increased or decreased appetite.
3. Sleep problems, either insomnia or hypersomnia.
4. Psychomotor agitation or retardation.
5. Loss of interest in formerly pleasurable things.
6. Loss of energy and excessive fatigue.
7. Feelings of worthlessness, self-reproach, or excessive, inappropriate guilt.
8. Complaints or evidence of diminished ability to concentrate, slowed thinking, or indecisiveness.
9. Persistent and pervasive depressive thinking, including thoughts of death, suicidal ideation, wishes to be dead, or a suicide attempt.[2]

The above diagnostic criteria must be kept in mind when the counselor interviews the child who is depressed. In order to fully evaluate the child, he or she also must have had a thorough physical examination to rule out specific medical problems which may cause depression in childhood. Some of the medical diagnoses that could cause such depression include thyroid disease, heart disease, kidney disease, and neurological disorders.

Also, as part of the evaluation, a good family history is necessary. Some families are predisposed genetically to develop depression. Children with a clinically depressed parent have an increased risk of developing a mood disorder themselves.[3] If parents are depressed, they and the child will need treatment.

Depression takes on a different face with each stage of child development. In infancy, depression seems to be related almost exclusively to the infant's loss of bonding attachment with the mother. Such infants often are described as having anaclitic depression. Symptoms include listlessness, a sad face, lack of responsiveness to the environment even in a feeding situation, and possibly eating and sleeping disturbances. Experts have interpreted these symptoms to mean that the infant is withdrawing from a world made painful by the absence of bonding with the child's mother. They also have interpreted this to mean the child is deprived of needed environmental stimulation.

Reports of depression in children during the preschool years are few. This is believed to be related to the developmental characteristics of this stage. Small children do not sustain moods for long periods of time but react to change situations.

In middle childhood, from ages six to eight years, the findings of dysphoria, sadness, or even frank depression may occur more frequently. Children of this age can be profoundly sad because of events in their environment. This probably has to do with their cognitive structure, which primarily is based on intuition rather than on looking beyond the immediate situation to logically understand what is happening. Their feelings are tied to a concrete, immediate, and present environment. During this developmental phase, the child generally idealizes his or her parents. The child needs the parents' positive response to help resolve sad feelings.

Sometime after the eighth year of life, the child begins to show a more classic picture of depression. This is when the child begins to develop a system of thinking that includes evaluating the self and others. Therefore, a dysphoric or depressed response follows trauma or crises in the environment. By now, this response includes a sense of personal failure or perhaps disappointment with others and the child begins to verbalize a sense of worthlessness or even guilt as part of the depressed-symptom picture.

Children of this age can become depressed when events occurring within the family leave them feeling worthless. For example, they may feel unable to please their parents. Similarly, they can become depressed when they feel worthless in a context outside the home—with teachers, parents' friends, or with other significant adults in their lives.

Once a child reaches adolescence, at about age eleven or twelve, a further dimension is added to the depression. Besides all of the other symptoms—the sad or depressed response to a specific crisis, the feeling of self-worthlessness, guilt, and self-deprecation—now the young person begins to predict that the future always will be bleak and painful. Because of this, seemingly minor events, such as failing a test at school or breaking up with a boyfriend or girlfriend, can cause the adolescent serious depression. Further discussion of adolescent depression and suicide is part of the companion volume, *Counseling and Adolescents.* [4]

Treating depression is as multifaceted in children as it is in adults. The following components are necessary:

1. *Accurate diagnosis.* As just discussed, diagnosing depression in children and adolescents can be difficult, since they do not always present symptoms of primary sadness, tearfulness, or feelings of desolation. Frequently they can show depressed feelings, but their behaviors will be explosiveness or disruptiveness, as well as sadness, withdrawal, and tearfulness. In light of this, children with any kinds of abnormal or disruptive behavior should be considered for childhood depression diagnosis.

2. *Individual therapy with the child.* A crucial element in this therapy is developing a close, empathic, and trusting relationship between the child and the therapist. From this relationship, the child can restructure his or her view of the world and find answers to the conflicts leading to the depressed feelings.

The child also can receive a corrective emotional experience from this counselor-patient relationship. The counselor can offer an experience of empathy, warmth, and acceptance and at the same time provide guidelines and suggestions for changes in behavior and in the child's world view.

The counselor-patient relationship also allows the child to vent his or her feelings and thoughts. Being able to vent worries, fears, sadness, anger, hopelessness, and conflict in a safe environment and within a safe relationship helps externalize these feelings. This allows for emotional growth.

3. *Family therapy.* The family should be involved in the therapeutic process, since a problem at any level in the system is a problem for all the system. This involvement may directly center on the child's difficulties and on the family's response, or may also include other troubles between parents or between parents and other children. The goal of this family therapy is that the child ultimately could vent feelings in the family setting as he or she does initially in the counselor-child relationship.

4. *Parent therapy.* As noted earlier, depressed children frequently have at least one parent who also is depressed. Therapy is crucial for parents who are depressed.

5. *Medication.* Within the last twenty years, several studies have documented the effectiveness of using tricyclic antidepressants in children.[5] The most commonly used antidepressant probably is Tofranil. These medications work by correcting altered levels of neurotransmitters in the limbic system of the brain. While antidepressant therapy frequently helps in treating the depressed child, it must be only a part of the treatment regime, along with individual and family therapy.

6. *Hospitalization.* The counselor should consider hospitalization for the depressed child when the child is so depressed he or she cannot function. This occurs when the child has excessive trouble with fatigue, is unable to attend school or to care for oneself or to cope with overwhelming thoughts of sadness, including suicidal ideation and/or attempts.

Working with depressed children sometimes seems like a monumental task, but with a good treatment regime the prognosis is quite good. An aggressive, well-rounded treatment approach will prevent many problems down the road for the depressed child.

THE FEARFUL AND ANXIOUS CHILD

One of Carrie's favorite stories was about a toy fire engine that longed to fight big fires like real fire engines do. In the story, the department store where the toy fire engine lived eventually caught fire, and the little engine was able to stop a tiny blaze that endangered hundreds of people.

Each time Carrie went to bed, she begged her parents to read this book to her. Soon, however, Carrie awakened during the night, saying she was afraid of fire. Even watching her parents build a fire in the fireplace could suddenly prompt Carrie to cry in terror.

The magic and fantasy that create such excitement in the child's world can also be a source of childhood fears, as the fanciful book became in Carrie's case.

One recent survey of a thousand children found that approximately 90 percent between ages 2 and 14 had a specific phobia or fear. In another study, 43 percent of children between 6 and 12 reported they had significant fears and worries.[6]

Because childhood fears are so pervasive, deciding which fears need or warrant a counselor's treatment can be difficult. Generally, it can be said that fears which consistently inhibit normal daily activities are those that require intervention by a counselor.

Identifying abnormal fears requires some understanding of what constitutes *normal* fears in the child. A newborn's primary fears are loud noises and falling. From six months to a year, the child begins to have some fear of strangers, which often lasts until age two or three. At age one, the child becomes reluctant to go to strangers and is apprehensive about separating from parents. This fear may last up to seven or eight years of age.

Children in the preschool age bracket often fear a variety of things—the dark, the "boogeyman," supernatural creatures, sleeping alone, animals, or anything large and foreboding. Children in the grade-school years may have more socially relevant fears, such as a fear of intruders in the home, nuclear war, embarrassment at school, or failing a grade. In the adolescent years, teen-agers' fears pertain to self-worth anxieties, peergroup acceptance, and intimacy concerns. Most of these generally are not long in duration and are relatively mild.

The following seven fears and disorders represent the variety of anxieties facing the grade-school child.

1. *Simple fear or phobia.* These kinds of fears often come and go during the grade-school-age years. As long as they do not persist or impair the child's adaptation capabilities, or social or emotional development, they need not be cause for serious concern. Earlier in this book we discussed the "E.A.R.S. for

Fears" approach* which counselors can share with parents regarding phobias.

2. *Separation anxiety.* This anxiety is more worrisome; it represents the child's concern that some calamity will happen if the child is away from his or her parents. In younger children, this is a vague sense of apprehension and anxiety; in older children, this may relate to a specific incident, such as kidnapping or a heart attack. Tony, eight, developed separation anxiety after several traumatic events happened while he was away from his family. When he was six, he was the only member of his family not present when the house burned. The next year, he was visiting a cousin when a hurricane damaged the family residence. He began to believe his absences brought harm to the family and feared leaving the family behind to go anywhere, even to a friend's home to play. In such instances, separation anxiety can be quite incapacitating.

3. *School refusal.* A child's refusal to go to school because of fearfulness is a true problem. These children are different from truant youngsters who are relatively unbothered by fears and who simply have other, more enjoyable activities in mind rather than attending school. Occasionally, school refusal is a true fear or phobia that is related to a specific part of the school experience. When we think about it, we can see that children are called upon in school to participate in at least four activities which they are not obliged to carry out in other settings. (a) They have to mingle with some social acumen among their peers without parental supervision; (b) they must submit to rules that are established for the group; (c) they experience comparison with and competition against their peers; (d) they are exposed to the prospect of failure, and of feeling worthless should failure happen.

Monty, ten, had always found school a delightful place. But after his family moved to a new town, Monty suddenly began refusing to get out of bed and dress for school in the morning. Or, on days when he arrived at school, he soon ended up in the nurse's office complaining of a stomach ache, prompting the nurse to call his parents and send him home.

---

*See E.A.R.S. for Fears, page 28.

In counseling with their son, his parents learned that Monty's school refusal occurred because he had switched from a more relaxed school setting to one that emphasized competition at every turn. Monty was not used to being compared with peers on a regular basis. He feared he would constantly come up short in this setting, so he opted not to attend.

In other instances, children are more apprehensive about leaving home than they are fearful of going to school. This anxiety pertains specifically to the parent-child bond.

4. *Avoidant disorder of childhood.* This disorder refers to children who are painfully shy and literally go to any lengths to avoid contact with others, especially strangers. This shyness seems to persist even after lengthy exposure to people and occurs beyond the age when a normal fear of strangers would occur. The disorder is most commonly seen in children ages five through seven and seems to appear more frequently in girls than in boys.

Children with avoidant disorder actually shrink from strangers, cling to their parents, become silent, and usually display regressive behaviors characteristic of a much younger child.

5. *The overanxious disorder.* This sometimes is called the generalized anxiety disorder of childhood and is largely found in young people from homes with high performance expectations. These tend to be children from smaller families, usually of somewhat high socioeconomic class. They worry excessively about meeting other people's expectations for them and are prone to self-doubt. Also, they may be more self-conscious than other children.

This disorder is distributed equally among boys and girls and persists longer than does an adjustment disorder, in which a child deals with a major change or significant loss. Not linked clearly to a precipitating event, this disorder may have many characteristics in common with the separation anxiety disorder.

6. *The obsessive-compulsive disorder.* This disorder is marked by symptoms of repetitive thoughts, compulsive actions, and a sometimes fanatic adherence to a scheduled regimen of behaviors. These behaviors are designed to relieve somehow what the young person often perceives as a rather irrational fear.

The "role" of the obsessive-compulsive behavior is to reduce anxiety, shifting the child's concerns about an unthinkable thought or an unacceptable emotion.

For example, a child who feels he or she has done something dirty or nasty may start a compulsive ritual of hand-washing. The child believes this will somehow get rid of the residual guilt and shame. Obsessive-compulsive disorders also are seen frequently in adults. In a survey completed in 1984, fully one-third of adults with obsessive-compulsive disorder reported that it had been with them from childhood.[7]

7. *Post-traumatic stress disorder* (or adjustment disorder). Children who suddenly are forced to deal with substantial stress in their lives may develop a cadre of specific fears and unnamed anxieties. This is a normal phenomenon during a significant adjustment period. Symptoms of this disorder are lingering fears, panic episodes, irritability, inability to concentrate, chronic self-image distortions, fear of trusting others, pessimism, a sense of vulnerability, eating disturbances, allergies, and sleep problems. Because of these fears, the child tends to regress to earlier, "safer" ages of emotional development. The fears may have been activated from the child's past or simply infused by the circumstances and emotions surrounding the traumatic event the child encountered.

As mentioned above, in dealing with childhood fears and anxieties, we use the "E.A.R.S. for Fears" acrostic to help parents and caregivers. Counselors may want to refer to our discussion on this on pages 28–29, and apply that to the grade-school child.

Structuring activities that help guide children into nonthreatening and confidence-building interactions are therapeutically wise. Sometimes, letting children play with younger children with whom they have confidence and working them into more peer-appropriate interactions can help.

It is normally wise to introduce fearful children to new situations gradually. It is hard for children to begin overcoming fears when they are constantly barraged with new or intimidating experiences, such as school activities, sports try-outs, dancing classes, birthday parties, or church activities.

Molly's parents wanted the seven-year-old to overcome her fear of spending the night away from home. They did this by incremental steps. First, the parents left home overnight and invited Molly's grandparents to stay at the house with her. Next, Molly spent a night at her grandparents' house. Then, she stayed overnight with an aunt. After these three successes, Molly was confident enough to sleep over with a friend the next time she was invited.

A good track coach knows how to pace a young runner to maximize the conditioning effect. Likewise, a wise counselor and/or parents will pace the fearful or shy child to gradually expose him or her to more interpersonally rigorous experiences.

As we have mentioned before, the goal is not to push the child into some preconceived track or timetable of social achievement. Instead, the goal is to enhance the child's capacity to progress at his or her own pace through the developmental stages and to conquer the various fears that often pop up during the process.

Time, commitment, sensitivity, common sense, and the help of a good professional counselor in tough cases will resolve childhood fears and anxieties in most instances.

CHAPTER THIRTEEN

CO-DEPENDENCY, CHILD ABUSE, AND THE DYSFUNCTIONAL FAMILY

EVEN IN ELEMENTARY SCHOOL, Eric understood that his father consumed alcoholic beverages in excessive amounts. But Eric loved his father and tried to understand the role that all of his father's "problems" at work, at home, and seemingly everywhere played in the drinking.

After his mother died, Eric, by then in junior high school, became the emotional support for his father. When his dad came home late at night after too many drinks, Eric dutifully put him to bed, then called his father's employer the next morning to explain that his father was too ill to come to work that day.

Even at such a tender age, Eric took on the role of managing the house and cleaning up after his father. Eventually he got a job to help his dad make ends meet.

Now, as an adult, Eric moves from job to job where he ends up in a back-up role to a top executive who has creative ideas but can't keep his company or office running smoothly. Eric steps in and wins applause for his ability to keep the operation functioning efficiently.

With the help of counseling in his early twenties, Eric came to understand the role his father's alcoholism played in leading him to become a tower of support and strength virtually everywhere he goes. Though his outcome has worked to his advantage, Eric is not alone in this co-dependency role. Frequently, a parent's problems complicate life for their children.

Co-dependency, a popular term in current literature, is "an emotional, psychological and behavioral condition that develops as a result of an individual's prolonged exposure to and practice of a set of oppressive rules . . . rules which prevent the open expression of feelings as well as the direct discussion of personal and interpersonal problems."[1] Another writer describes the co-dependent person as "one who has let another person's behavior affect him or her, and who is obsessed with controlling that person's behavior."[2]

Co-dependency also has been described as an enmeshment of one's identity and the identity of another. It involves assuming responsibility for another's needs to the exclusion of one's own. Under the general "umbrella" of co-dependency, we would list these characteristics:

- A tendency to excessively rely on denial
- Constriction of emotions (with or without dramatic outburst)
- Problems with anxiety and/or depression
- Hypervigilance
- Compulsions
- Substance abuse or impulse dyscontrol
- "Setting oneself up" as a recurrent victim of physical abuse (including sexual abuse) and stress-related medical illness.

These have been eloquently described by Timmen Cermak in an article, "Diagnosing and Treating Co-Dependence."[3]

THE TYPES OF DYSFUNCTIONAL
FAMILY SYSTEMS

Five types of dysfunctional family systems contribute to co-dependent behavior in children. They are the following:

1. The family in which one or both parents are actively involved in substance addiction or abuse is a spawning ground for co-dependent behavior. Considering the extent of drug abuse in North America, the likelihood of a counselor encountering families in which drugs or alcohol are taking an emotional toll is very high. Sixty percent of the adult population of the United States uses alcohol. In that group are some 12 million alcoholics. Among American teen-agers, about 5 percent of high-school seniors use alcohol daily; approximately 4 million teen alcoholics exist.

Perhaps more than ever, the special problems of adult children of alcoholics are being recognized today. That subject is the theme of a separate volume in the Resources for Christian Counseling series.* Author Janet Woititz has singled out some of the various traits and attitudes characteristic of children raised in dysfunctional homes. These are:

a. The children are confused as to what "normal" is.
b. They have difficulty completing projects or tasks.
c. They lie compulsively, even when there is no need to.
d. They are overly critical of themselves.
e. They take themselves too seriously and have difficulty having fun.
f. As adults they have difficulty with intimate relationships. They struggle for intimacy.
g. There is a great need for control of one's life and excessive anger when this control cannot be achieved.
h. There is a lifelong need for approval and affirmation.
i. There is a feeling of being different from other people (somehow "damaged goods").

Counseling Adult Children of Alcoholics, by Sandra D. Wilson, Ph.D., vol. 21 in the Resources for Christian Counseling Series (Dallas: Word, 1989).

j. They are overly responsible in their conduct; or, the reverse, they are overly irresponsible in their conduct.

k. There is extreme loyalty to the perpetrators of abuse or primary characters in the dysfunctional family even though it is unwarranted.

l. There is a high frequency of impulsive behavior which only aggravates existing problems.[4]

Sixty million people in the United States have tried marijuana, and eighteen to twenty-five million use it regularly. At least twenty-five million people have tried cocaine, and an estimated six million people are regular users. Several million people in the United States regularly take amphetamines, tranquilizers, and sleeping pills. Add to this the narcotic pain medications and legal tranquilizers prescribed by the multiplied thousands each year, and it is no wonder that the ravages of drug abuse show up so frequently in American families, church-going or not.[5]

2. The psychologically disturbed family system, in which one or more family members suffer from significant emotional illness, is seen as another setting where co-dependent relationships develop. Families that experience a major depressive disorder, especially recurrent depressions in either spouse, or in which there is a schizophrenic disorder, are at risk for the development of co-dependent behavior in children.

3. Co-dependency is also seen in families having especially harsh or rigidly dogmatic rules. Unfortunately, some well-meaning Christian families fall into this category. Later in this chapter we will look at some of the family rules seen in the dysfunctional homes of co-dependent children. Counselors will observe that these rules tend to show up in unhealthy, dogmatic family systems.

Substance abuse contributes to co-dependency because the substance becomes a replacement for a relationship for the abuser. Gratification, joy, and problem solving all begin to be found in a substance rather than in a relationship. Because the healthy relationship is gone, others around the substance abuser may take on the responsibility of solving the abuser's problems without confronting the real problem, in order to keep "peace at any price." In other words, the co-dependent person now seeks gratification, joy, and problem solving in co-dependency rather than a healthy relationship where there are clear and healthy boundaries.

4. The sexually abusive or physically abusive home is another setting where co-dependent behavior in children might be found. Children trapped in such homes often develop a variety of co-dependent behaviors simply as a means of survival.

The American Humane Association has issued a sobering collection of statistics pertaining to physical and sexual abuse in the United States. According to the association's report, one in four girls and one in ten boys under age eighteen will be victims of sexual abuse by an adult, and two to five children will die each day from some form of abuse. Some of the more poignant findings are:

- The average age of the child victim of abuse is seven years.
- Perhaps 70 percent of runaways are actually fleeing an abusive home environment.
- 80 percent of the prisoners in jails and penitentiaries were abused as children.
- 97 percent of the hard-core delinquents have a history of child abuse.
- 80 percent of prostitutes were sexually abused as children.[6]

In Figure 13-1, signs of sexual abuse in children are given as a means of aiding the counselor in determining the presence of sexual abuse.

The first four of these family systems, all of which can be highly prone to the development of co-dependent behavior in children, have been described by Robert Subby in his book *Lost in the Shuffle.*[7]

5. The family in which "emotional incest" occurs is also a place where co-dependency develops in children. By "emotional incest" is meant a condition of an unhealthy bond between parent and child, not as a result of sexual abuse but as a consequence of an inappropriate relationship between parent and child. This condition can result from a combination of characteristics from one or more of the first four types of dysfunctional families. Yet, in our practices we have seen enough

The characteristics of child sexual abuse are varied. If a counselor sees several of these symptoms, sexual abuse may be suspected.

1. A child experiencing pain or itching in the genital area; walking or sitting with difficulty.
2. A female whom the physician finds to be bruised or bleeding in the external vaginal or anal areas.
3. A female with a history of vaginal discharge or unexplained venereal disease.
4. A child with encopresis or recurrent urinary-tract infection.
5. A child showing precocious or unusually advanced sexual behavior or knowledge inappropriate for the child's age.
6. A child showing poor peer relationships and systematic low self-esteem.
7. A child who suddenly has problems in school and who may have adopted changed eating and sleeping habits.
8. A child who is fearful of adults, especially men.
9. A child's whose exploitation seems encouraged by the parents, or whose home is known to be a setting for drug and alcohol abuse.
10. Low self-esteem in the parents and a history of violent or angry outbursts at home by one or more parents.
11. A family with significant financial or marital problems which are seen to negatively affect the father in the home.
12. A child who develops antisocial, delinquent, or runaway behavior patterns.

Figure 13–1
Warning Signs for Sexual Abuse

families to warrant its being recognized independently of the others.

There are four general types of emotional incest.

a. One is a situation in which parents are guilty of overparenting; these are the ones who control too much, threatening to emotionally suffocate the child.

b. The opposite is the underattentive parent who is too busy and too distracted by other commitments or activities to give the child proper psychological and emotional attention. This parent is detached. The child seeks to spend inordinate amounts of time with the parent, idolizing him or her to win affection, attention, and approval. The child can almost lose his or her own identity in this pursuit.

c. A third form of emotional incest, when the child must "parent" the parent, occurs when the parent is struggling due to stresses. These may be brought on by drug abuse, a debilitating physical illness, chronic depression, or a recent divorce. In such cases, the child actually assumes a strong emotional posture and becomes the caretaker of the parent.

Amy's situation may serve us as an example. She was born and raised by a teen-age mom, whose marriage lasted only a brief while. As her mother became incapable of coping with life, Amy found herself assuming the role of parent to her scatter-brained, emotionally immature mother. As a result, Amy never knew a normal, carefree childhood.

d. There are some families in which a child is put in the position of a missing parent; it might be said the child is "married" to the remaining parent. The child essentially takes the place of a missing or nonfunctional parent. This can be seen, for example, after a divorce when a single-parent mother allows her son to essentially adopt many of the former husband's responsibilities and even try to meet many of her emotional needs. This can be a subtle thing. The child may perceive his or her role as "filling in" for the now-missing spouse. This places tremendous pressure upon such children involved who must essentially rechannel the direction of their emotional and psychological development to assume adult-like responsibilities.

Emerging from a dysfunctional home like one of the types mentioned here, the child will have developed some classic means of handling life's stresses. He or she will probably also adopt one of the following roles: the *enabler,* the *hero,* the *scapegoat,* the *lost child,* or the *mascot* of the family. These roles are adapted from Sharon Wegscheider-Cruse's book, *Another Chance: Hope and Health for the Alcoholic Family.* The actual abusing member of the family has a role as well. Figure 13-2 lists the five roles and describes what motivates each, what are the identifying symptoms and payoffs, and what the cost may be to each role player.

The "enabler" is usually a role taken by a key person in the

THE ROLE	MOTIVATING FEELING	IDENTIFYING SYMPTOMS	"PAYOFF" FOR INDIVIDUAL	"PAYOFF" FOR FAMILY	POSSIBLE PRICE
ENABLER	anger	powerlessness	importance self-righteousness	responsibility	illness, "martyrdom"
HERO	inadequacy guilt	overachievement	attention (positive)	self-worth	compulsive drive; workaholism as teens and adults
SCAPEGOAT	hurt	delinquency	attention (negative)	focus away from dependent	self-destruction, use of anger and intimidation to handle problems in life
LOST CHILD	loneliness	solitariness shyness	escape	relief	social isolation, a "doormat" adult later in life
MASCOT	fear	clowning hyperactivity	attention (amused)	fun	immaturity, emotional illness, master of deception

Figure 13–2

Roles in the Dysfunctional Family

family, such as Eric mentioned at the beginning of this discussion. This person feels compelled to try at all costs to minimize the chaos felt by the dysfunctional family members. Enablers sometimes function as sufferers; they try to reduce the level of family suffering by taking an undue measure upon themselves, and by eliciting an air of self-pity and martyrdom. They feel their actions somehow may cause the perpetrator to reduce the intensity of the abuse.

The enabler who acts as a punisher tries to reduce the family dysfunction by attacking individuals whom he or she feels may contribute to the abuse and dysfunction. The enabler who functions as a controller, as the name would imply, seeks to enlist the help of others to change situations so as to remove the element of the unpredictable. In general, the enabler orchestrates as many functions in the home as possible in an effort to reduce the dysfunctional behavior.

The family "hero" is the individual who either directly or indirectly assumes responsibility for the family's dysfunction. For example, if a father abuses his daughter sexually, the young girl may, as the hero, assume the sexual abuse is her fault. She may think if she were a better student, a more accomplished athlete, or a more astute pianist, somehow the abuse would stop. The family hero often becomes a superachiever and continually attempts to use his or her own personal achievement to stop the family's dysfunctional nature.

The family "scapegoat" is the victim who feels unwanted or unneeded in the family. The scapegoat typically feels like "damaged goods" and frequently resorts to rebellious or delinquent behavior. The scapegoat's hidden goal is to act out enough and to produce enough rejections so there is no need to face how dependent and needy he or she really is.

The "lost child," on the other hand, is the one who seeks to blend with the family and "cause no trouble." The lost child likes to "go with the flow" and may use physical and/or psychological retreat as a coping and defense mechanism against the dysfunctional experiences transpiring at home. The lost child is not one to "come out of his shell" and often presents the counselor with a particularly difficult case.

The "mascot" is the family's joker or clown. Mascots "succeed" in their role when they are able to divert the family's attention away from the intense anguish of its dysfunctional nature. Unfortunately, mascots often aren't sure just how to grow up. They rely on being pranksters, on being impish and joking to defuse the pain at home. Somehow in the shuffle of the developmental process, they end up being chronically childish and shallow people. They may make acquaintances easily on the surface but keep very few, if any, deep and long-lasting friendships.

The counselor asked to help a child struggling within a dysfunctional family should try to get the whole family into therapy. If this is not possible, the counselor should try to work with as many members as are willing.

Initially, the counselor aims at establishing a bond of trust, a climate in which family members can let their defenses down and honestly disclose their feelings. The counseling will involve the eliciting of some strong negative emotions. These may discourage the counselee. But once trust is established and emotions are being shared, both positive and negative, the counselor can suggest more healthy ways to think and behave. These new, healthy ways of thinking and behaving should cause emotions to normalize and the discouraging mood to lift.

The counselor should stress the lifelong nature of co-dependency. Family members will need to see that they must guard against the old patterns while continuing in a positive direction lest they relapse into co-dependent behavior. In many communities, support groups comprised of people who came out of dysfunctional families exist today. People involved in co-dependent relationships should consider participating in these as time permits.

COUNSELING FOR CO-DEPENDENCY

Counselors may not only be called upon directly to help co-dependent children. They may be asked to assist public school and Sunday school teachers, or others who work with children. The counselor will want to advise that structure, predictability, and stability be considered as priorities, so the child becomes accustomed to a routine and a schedule.

Arranging for socializing and peer involvements in which the child is likely to form new friendships can help the child overcome the isolation that often is a part of life in the dysfunctional family.

The counselor should try to bolster a child's self-esteem, using small successes and unsolicited praise to introduce counter-dependent thought processes and behavior patterns. A third grade teacher who taught Ben, the child of an alcoholic mother, appointed him as her classroom "secretary." The teacher asked Ben to monitor her schedule: what days she was assigned lunchroom duty, what days her class took up ice cream money, what days she monitored recess. The task filled Ben with pride as he helped the teacher remember her assigned duties and served to make up for the damage done to Ben's self-esteem.

A teacher, upon recognizing co-dependent behavior in a child, will want the child to sense that the classroom is a safe island where he or she feels more in control and capable of directing the course of the day's activity. This is in contrast to how the child feels in the emotional crucible of the dysfunctional home.

Counselors, either directly or indirectly, can give the child permission to really relish his or her childhood. Often, children from dysfunctional homes feel pressured to grow up in a hurry, to quit being foolish or childish. Dysfunctional homes seldom tolerate behaviors that don't coincide with the family's expressed wishes. The improbable, relaxed, impromptu antics of childhood sometimes are squelched in the dysfunctional home.

In Ben's case, the teacher relished the moments when she saw Ben running spiritedly in a soccer game on the school playground. She knew such frolicking moments were few in Ben's home, where he and his younger brother took on many adult responsibilities because their mother was incapacitated. The counselor should allow the co-dependent young person to put some zest back into playing and learning as a youngster.

Also, it is very important to offer the child hope. The counselor will want to help the child see that a safe path exists which can lead to emotional wholeness and maturity outside the vortex of the dysfunctional home. Sometimes children benefit from talking to adults who have come through similar experiences or from getting together in group sessions with children from similar homes. The counselor might be the catalyst for such a gathering. This can begin to open the child's eyes to the possibility of hope and can help break the pattern of recurrent dysfunctional living.

Counselors working with children from any of the five types of dysfunctional homes certainly have a challenge on their hands. The amount and depth of emotional scarring which a dysfunctional home can inflict in the personality make-up of a young child is staggering. Yet, God has designed persons to be wonderfully resilient.

ANTISOCIAL BEHAVIORS

During school-age years, many children develop antisocial behaviors. These behaviors defy the norms of society and often violate the rights of others.

In therapy, the counselor must be careful to look for depression and other underlying causes for these antisocial behaviors. Recent research shows that as many as 25 percent of children with antisocial behaviors are actually depressed. In this section we will discuss stealing, lying, cheating, bad language, fire setting, and truancy.

Stealing

For an incident to be called stealing, the child must have known that he or she was wrong to take the object without the owner's permission. Minor stealing incidents in early childhood are quite common. If three-year-old Stacy helps herself to one of the wrapped candies sold by the pound at the grocery store, her act is hardly cause for alarm.

As children develop a stronger structure of conscience, stealing gradually decreases and is essentially nonexistent in normal children. But children who continue to steal past early childhood can present major worries for the parents. If at age ten Stacy slips a bottle of nail polish into her purse as she stands at the cosmetic counter, this becomes a serious matter.

Children steal for a variety of reasons. Some are highly impulsive. While they know it is wrong to steal, the desire to own an object overcomes their consciences, and they steal.

Other children may steal because they feel they are missing out on something. In such cases, stealing becomes a symbolic replacement for the absence of something, perhaps parental love, attention, or affection. Still other children may steal to bolster their self-esteem—they feel the stolen items prove to others their toughness or their competence—or they steal in anger to get even with a parent.

Regardless of the reasons a child may steal, the counselor must immediately and directly intervene to extinguish that behavior. When a child has stolen, the parents should immediately take action rather than overlooking or minimizing the act. The parent needs to take time to talk to the child and try to understand why the child stole. At the same time, the child should correct this behavior by immediately returning the stolen item(s). If that is not possible, the parent should see that the child arranges to compensate for the stolen items.

It is important to immediately and consistently set the consequences for acts of stealing. Apologies, explanations, tears, and promises not to repeat the behavior should not be allowed to undermine the certainty of stealing's consequences. If such behavior persists, parents should seek therapy for the child to determine the underlying causes and to correct them.

Lying

Certainly all children lie, on occasion, but parents should regard honesty as an essential character trait above all others. Healthy relationships are based on this character trait. Lying is one of the most destructive forces in its effect on relationships.

A child's lying can take many forms. A lie can simply reverse the truth, or exaggerate, or be fabrication, in which the child tells a version of an event that is totally untrue, or be confabulation—telling something partly true and partly false.

Sometimes children lie to escape unpleasant consequences of behavior. Sometimes they lie to bolster their self-esteem with boasting and bragging. Sometimes the child's reality testing is impaired. At other times significant adults in the child's life have modeled lying.

Intervention for lying is similar to that of stealing. It must not be minimized. If a parent is sure a child has lied, a direct confrontation is in order. Asking the child why he has lied generally is unfruitful and actually may reinforce the child's lying behavior.

When Sarah's mother learned beyond a shadow of a doubt that Sarah had lied about not breaking a crystal candy dish which was a wedding present, the mother simply said, "Sarah, I am aware that you broke my candy dish. You lied to me earlier when I asked how it got broken. Because you lied, by this time tomorrow, I expect you to present me with a plan of how you are going to replace my broken dish."

In her comment, the mother stepped aside from a hairsplitting dispute over how the dish was broken. She merely confronted the child and then gave Sarah a deadline by which she would pay Mother back for the dish.

If the parent is uncertain, it's probably best not to confront, nor to try to ferret out whether the child has told the truth or not.

Throughout all this, the child must learn from the parent that truthfulness, indeed, is a virtue and that honesty and trust are the cornerstones and foundations of all healthy relationships. Counselor and parents should be aware that depression, poor self-esteem, or even an inaccurate understanding of reality may be at the root of the child's lying behavior.

Cheating

Cheating also is a common behavior in school-aged children. During the ages of eight to twelve, games with rules represent the preferred play activity of children. Because competition is keen in these games, children of this age believe in strictly adhering to the rules. Some children, however, find it difficult to accept defeat and generally will cheat at games as well as in the classroom.

Children generally cheat because they feel pressure for high classroom performance or because parents have a "win-at-any-cost" mentality. Other reasons center around a personality characteristic which dictates that the child cannot lose and will go to any cost to avoid losing because of the perceived damage to his or her self-esteem.

Because cheating is similar to lying, it creates mistrust, which destroys healthy relationships. Children must learn this hazard from an early age. To discourage cheating, parents should teach children that relationships are important and that classroom success or winning games is only secondary.

When the child is caught cheating, immediate consequences again are in order. It is best to use consequences which do not deride the child but which simply cause him or her to face the natural consequences of the action. This may include consequences of restitution.

Bad Language

Bad language in children generally falls into three categories: *profanity,* involving disrespect for something considered sacred or holy, such as the name of God; *cursing,* which reflects the wish to harm another person; or *obscenity,* referring to sex or bodily elimination in a joking, inappropriate, or sneering way.

School-age children use bad words either to get attention or for shock value. They also do this in an effort to assume superiority over other children or adults whom they make uncomfortable, or as a release of intense feelings and emotions.

In any case, the consistent use of bad language reflects a high level of insecurity in the child. Its appearance calls for the parent or counselor to use careful intervention into this child's feelings of self-worthlessness or helplessness.

Trey, ten, had been taught from early childhood the importance of not using swear words and especially of not taking God's name in vain. Trey attended Sunday school regularly and knew why such language was disrespectful to God. His parents were puzzled when Trey began taking God's name in vain on a repeated basis. As they observed this behavior, they noticed Trey only used profanity after he had had a bad day at school, such as incurring a teacher's displeasure or receiving a low grade on a test.

Certainly, consequences for using bad language need to be immediate and consistent. But parents also need to try to understand why children feel using bad words represents the only way they can gain acceptance or approval or express feelings. Children need to learn other ways of expressing feelings, particularly anger and frustration and feelings of worthlessness.

Parents should teach this in a relationship of care and concern and empathy.

In Trey's case, the parents tried to teach him to verbalize up front why he felt inadequate, to say, "I had a rough day at school today because I got a 60 on my test," rather than camouflage his true feelings behind a bluster of swear words.

Unfortunately, many children use bad language because adults model this sort of speech. It will be hard to change a child's bad language if the adults in that child's life consistently use bad language to cope with life situations.

Fire Setting

Watching fires and learning to fight fires and extinguish them is exciting and pleasurable for many children. But when a child repeatedly engages in this activity without parental supervision, there is cause for alarm.

Children who deliberately set fires pose a serious threat to their family and community. Because this behavior is obviously dangerous, correcting it must be a high priority for the counselor and the family.

Typically, the vast majority of fire setters are boys. One such youngster was Sam, a rural youngster who often delighted in setting fire to brush along the creek that bordered his family's rural acreage. At times he drew visiting friends into his misdeeds; at other times, he acted alone.

Fire setting may be a simple act, but its causes are many. These include poor impulse control—particularly the control of aggressive impulses—expression of unmet needs—such as loneliness and unhappiness—revenge, and a feeling that the father is not involved enough.

The latter was true with Sam. The youngster had learned a preoccupation with fire from his father, a firefighter with the city's fire department. Sam also had learned that his setting fires was a way to get his father's attention. When he repeatedly set fire to the creekbank, endangering surrounding property, he definitely snared his father's involvement, but in a negative way.

The typical profile of the fire-setting child is one of a lonely child with poor self-esteem who lacks healthy skills for dealing with his aggressive and angry impulses.

Intervening with a fire-setting child should be immediate and firm. The parents must put adequate limits on the child immediately and make an effort to determine the root causes of the fire-setting behavior. Sometimes these children should be referred to hospitals or to residential treatment facilities which can provide adequate structure and supervision and limits to prevent this child's fire-setting behavior from becoming a menace to family or community.

Truancy

Experimental truancy, or "playing hooky"—absenting oneself from school without a legitimate reason and without permission—is a common behavior among school-age children. However, when the behavior persists, parents and their truant children should be concerned. School truancy frequently is linked to poor school performance and a delinquent behavior tendency.

A child's absence from school may be due to parental indifference toward school. Unfortunately, many times a parent needs the child at home to do housework or baby-sitting, so the child is kept home from school.

Truant behavior may be due to the child's repeated frustration and even failure at school work. The child would rather avoid school work than face constant rejection and failure. On the other hand, the child may be bored with school work because he or she is intellectually too advanced for the class. This rarely causes truancy, but it does exist. Sometimes truancy occurs because the child fears the violence of bullies or school gangs.

But probably the most common cause of truancy is a child's antisocial behavior and seeking for excitement. Such children have trouble mastering delayed gratification, so truancy instantly gives them the thrill they seek.

Again, intervention should be immediate and consistent. It is imperative that the school and the parents impose natural consequences. Children who are consistently truant should be evaluated for learning disabilities and emotional problems. The school also may need to begin special programs geared to helping such children, with school problems and avoiding truancy.

Many schools have installed a "warmline" to help keep a check on truancy. The school gives parents a telephone number to call if their child has to miss school. A half-hour after school opens, a parent volunteer checks that day's warmline messages against teachers' attendance rolls. The volunteer calls the parent of any student reported absent but not reported on the warmline. In this way, parents are soon made aware if their child is truant.

Truancy frequently signals other antisocial behaviors or emotional disturbances. These root causes should be identified and addressed.

Antisocial behaviors are, indeed, difficult for the counselor to deal with. These behaviors must be seen as warning signs of significant behavioral, developmental, or family problems. Resolving them will require the counselor to work persistently with both the child and the family.

CHAPTER FOURTEEN

CHILDREN WITH HABIT DISORDERS, CHRONIC ILLNESSES, AND HANDICAPS

SHAWN WAS A PERKY, GREGARIOUS seven-year-old who read and did math like she was an eleven-year-old. A straight-A student, she wrote poetry with a maturity far beyond her years. However, Shawn had a habit disorder that kept her at a toddler's maturity level in one area of her life. Every morning, Shawn awoke with a wet bed. She had a habit called nocturnal enuresis, which involves a child age five or older who is unable to contain urine while he or she sleeps.

ENURESIS

Nocturnal enuresis is one of the problems termed habit disorders because they occur frequently and repetitively. Besides nocturnal enuresis, these disorders include soiling (encopresis) and tic disorders. Other habit disorders such as thumb-sucking and nail-biting were mentioned in earlier chapters.

Nocturnal enuresis differs from diurnal enuresis (daytime wetting), which usually occurs when a child, excited or busy at play, does not respond to the stimulation of a full bladder in time to avoid incontinence.

Even at age 7, at least 10 percent of boys and about 3 percent of girls still experience nocturnal enuresis.[1] Enuresis in children and even adolescents is a chronic condition with an excellent long-term but a poor short-term prognosis. While most children by ages 4 or 5 achieve urinary continence, a significant number of people still have nocturnal enuresis during childhood and even well into adolescence.

Two kinds of enuresis occur: primary, meaning that the child regardless of age has never obtained any significant urinary continence at night, and secondary, a reoccurrence of nocturnal enuresis after a period of sustained urinary continence.

Secondary enuresis frequently coincides with some stressful event in the child's life, such as birth of a sibling, admission to the hospital, starting school, family stress and tension, or physical or sexual abuse. Experts generally agree that secondary enuresis indicates a possible psychological basis, while primary enuresis probably has a neurological base best described as immature bladder control.

Children with frequent nocturnal enuresis seem to have a low functional bladder volume, which means they may have urinary frequency and urgency during the day. It also seems many enuretic children are dry when they sleep away from home, are on vacation, or stay with a friend. A careful history taken from these children usually indicates they are dry because they have kept themselves awake hoping to avoid the embarrassment of bedwetting.

A small percentage of children with nocturnal enuresis also have daytime wetting. An even smaller percentage have associated urinary-tract abnormalities or urinary-tract infections. Although experts don't understand exactly why this occurs, they generally believe most children with enuresis have the problem because the bladder sphincter muscles are late in maturing.

Many surveys show that psychiatric symptoms are more common among children who are bedwetters than among those who are not bedwetters.[2]

Two main reasons possibly explain the association between enuresis and behavioral disturbance. The first is that enuresis is, indeed, a distressing condition. Possibly, any associated disturbance is a result directly of the bedwetting itself. Children who are chronic bedwetters usually are distressed by the problem. Therefore, it makes sense that they are at higher risk for anxiety and depression and even acting-out behavior disorders.

The second explanation of the significant association between enuresis and behavior disturbance is in the psychodynamic literature suggesting that enuresis itself is a sign of psychopathology. Specifically, this thinking comes from the theory that enuresis is a covert manifestation of aggression in children with passive-dependent personality characteristics.[3]

However, little research evidence supports this psychodynamic theory. In fact, most evidence points to the importance of biological rather than psychodynamic factors as a cause for enuresis. Besides bladder immaturity noted above, other biological evidence includes the high incidence of general neurological immaturity. Also frequently, family histories show that about 25 percent of enuretics have a close relative who also was enuretic.[4]

It also is likely, however, that certain experiences may predispose a child to become or remain incontinent. Some of these experiences include being hospitalized between the ages of one and three years, being residents of child-care institutions, and being a child of a severely dysfunctional family. Some theories also relate nocturnal enuresis to poor or inadequate training of bladder muscles during the early period of toilet training.

Evaluating a child with nocturnal enuresis should begin with a full medical evaluation, which includes a careful physical exam, urinalysis, and urine culture. If bacteria show up in the urine, the physician may order certain x-ray studies to view the urinary tract. A doctor then takes a careful medical history. The history determines the enuresis's frequency and determines whether enuresis is related to any family or childhood crisis.

The physician also should ask the parents what types of management they have tried in the past for the condition. Parents usually say they have tried limiting fluids, waking the child in the middle of the night for bathroom visits, and offering rewards or punishments, respectively, for nighttime dryness or wetness.

In the case of Shawn, the seven-year-old mentioned previously, her parents punished her by refusing to allow her to spend the night with friends until she began waking up dry on a continuing basis. However, as with Shawn, these rewards or punishment often do not work, since a wet bed seems to bring out anger in most parents.

Other items in the history will involve (1) any evidence of primary behavioral or emotional disorders, (2) the child's feeling about enuresis, (3) or any medication previously used.

It is important to tell the child that many other children have enuresis and that the long-term outlook is very good for children with this condition. This information makes many of them feel better. Sometimes the therapist will ask the child to keep a calendar record of dry nights and wet nights. This in and of itself encourages the child to decrease or even stop the enuresis. During this stage of treatment, the therapist should help the child understand that enuresis is not a behavior over which the child has conscious control. Indeed, it is an unpleasant habit disorder that can be treated.

A second way to treat enuresis is to have the parents awaken the child during the night to empty his or her bladder. These common-sense kinds of measures frequently cure the problem of enuresis.

The physician sometimes can treat enuresis surgically. The most common procedure involves dilatation of the urinary tract, if the enuresis is caused by obstruction in the urinary outflow tract. However, this treatment no longer is recommended. While psychotherapy may help deal with the secondary problems of enuresis such as depression, anxiety, and embarrassment, psychotherapy alone is not an effective treatment for enuresis.

Recently, medication therapy has been used and has been at least temporarily successful in many enuretic children. The most commonly used medications are tricyclic antidepressants. Exactly how these medicines act is unclear, but their activity does follow a consistent pattern. Generally within the first week the child takes the medicine, the enuresis decreases; but it relapses within four to six weeks despite increasing the medication dosage. Most experts do not recommend medication treatment for enuresis except in cases in which the child needs some quick intervention to stop enuresis for events like spending the night with a friend or going on a camping trip.

The most effective treatment for enuresis involves using the Mowrer apparatus known as the bell and pad. This behavioral conditioning treatment offers a good prospect for permanent cure. However, it is time-consuming and demanding of the patient, the family, and ultimately the therapist. Parents install the system in the child's bed, where two metal plates conduct electricity. When the child urinates in bed, an alarm sounds. The system seems to work both in a classic conditioning manner and also in an avoidance-learning manner. This method is an effective treatment for enuresis in children.[5]

ENCOPRESIS

After Danny had learned to use the toilet for his bowel movements, his parents were overly harsh and punitive when he had accidents. They spanked him hard several times a day when he failed to reach the toilet in time, and they scolded him by saying, "Danny dirtied his diaper. Bad Danny," much in the way one speaks to an animal.

It was no wonder, then, that as he entered first grade, Danny still had the habit of encopresis, or fecal soiling in the child's clothing. Fecal soiling after four years of age is not considered normal.

While encopresis is not as common as is enuresis, it is not rare. The problems associated with a child having encopresis can be overwhelming. The obvious frustration and rejection the child experiences can have long-lasting psychological effects.

Primary encopresis occurs when soiling continues after age four with no significant period of fecal continence. Secondary encopresis occurs when soiling happens after a significant period of bowel control.

Poor parenting practices during the toilet training period, as occurred with Danny's parents, represent one thing that can cause encopresis. The first is thought to be poor or inadequate bowel training during the toilet-training period. Sometimes the child has a neurological disorder or some degree of mental retardation that impairs the child's toilet training. This cause for encopresis is relatively rare.

A second type of encopresis occurs when the child has clearly attained toilet training but continues to pass feces in socially inappropriate settings. In these cases, a discernible pattern to the soiling behavior occurs in specific settings or in specific stressful situations. Coercive toilet-training practices may contribute to this type of soiling. The child with this type of encopresis frequently lacks distress over the soiling symptoms. This type of encopresis also is relatively rare.

The most common kind of encopresis actually occurs because of the child's overretention of fecal material. The child does this because of coercive or punitive toilet training already mentioned, because of experiences with painful bowel movements, or because of passive-aggressive power struggles between the child and parent. Eventually a large mass of fecal material collects in the child's colon. In turn, the child's colon becomes dysfunctional because of the large mass. The child then leaks watery stool material and soils his or her pants.

A physician familiar with encopretic children should conduct a thorough physical examination. The physician should take a careful history to determine which kind of encopresis occurs. The doctor also should assess the child's emotional and behavioral characteristics as well as review the family system. It is important that the physician rule out physiological abnormalities causing the symptoms of encopresis. Other important information includes a careful history of toilet training, behavioral and personality traits of the child, and learning how the child feels about the problem.

Treatment for encopresis is tedious and can be long-term. It is best managed by a therapist working with a physician who is interested in the problem.

In the most common forms of encopresis, a fecal-treatment plan is initiated first. This includes a series of enemas designed to empty the colon of the huge fecal mass. If this is not done, the colon cannot function normally and no success can occur. Then the bowel must be retrained. This occurs by setting up specific times for the child to sit on the toilet. The physician may prescribe suppositories to stimulate the colon to empty itself. At the same time, the child should begin a behavior-modification plan. This includes a star chart with stars for soil-free days and no stars for soiling days. The child later redeems these stars for a positive social-interaction event with a parent or other special person in the family.

The child receives no overt punishment for soiling. However, natural consequences of soiling involve washing one's clothes, taking a bath, and cleaning up one's self.

Psychotherapy with these children needs to help them identify feelings, particularly anger and dependency feelings, and to find better ways of dealing with those feelings. This therapy also should include the family, since family members are involved in the behavior-management plan and in the interpersonal conflicts and power struggles in which encopretic children find themselves.

TIC DISORDERS

Abrupt, repetitive, nonpurposeful body movements, in which the muscles move in an involuntary, impulsive, but persistent manner are tic disorders. Typical ones include eye blinking, facial and neck twitches, and shoulder movements. Tics also may involve the extremities and the trunk. Vocal tics are repeated noises or phrases. Mild nervous ticks frequently occur in children who tend to be anxious and shy. Nervous tics or habit tics tend to become more intense and frequent during stress, but during sleep they do not appear.

Treating habit tics involves teaching the child to decrease tension, and helping the family identify situations producing anxiety in the child and decreasing those or the anxiety associated with the situations. It also involves generally ignoring the habit tic itself.

A physician should evaluate any child having a tic that persists longer than two weeks. This is done to rule out other serious neurological disease, especially Tourette's syndrome. Tourette's syndrome is a neurological disease, not a psychiatric one, that consists of the following constellation of symptoms. (1) It is a muscular tic primarily over the face or neck. However, it can occur over the extremities or over the body. (2) It is a phonic or vocal tic, which may involve throat clearing, whining, wheezing, snorting, or grunting. (3) *Coprolialia*—a behavior of blurting out obscene words occurs sometimes in children who develop Tourette's syndrome. This particular behavior is quite disturbing to the family and in the classroom. (4) Present is an agitated, distractible, impulsive personality pattern similar to that of a child with attention deficit disorder.

Tourette's syndrome can be diagnosed accurately only by history of the symptoms previously listed. Most of the symptoms need to be present for at least six months to a year before the Tourette's diagnosis is made. These symptoms generally occur in the eighth or ninth year. Some children start with just the facial tics and never progress past that point. In others the frequency of initial tics steadily increases. Later, the phonic tics and coprolialia develop, with typical personality and behavior patterns accompanying them.

If the child is diagnosed with Tourette's syndrome, the next step may be medical management. The most common medications used are antipsychotic medicines such as Haldol, or, in recent years, Orap. Since medications have many side effects, a qualified physician must monitor them. Parents should monitor closely the emotional needs of the child with Tourette's syndrome. Such children usually become angry at the syndrome and embarrassed about their tic symptoms.

Recently, experts have discovered that many children with Tourette's syndrome in the past have been wrongly diagnosed as having attention deficit disorder. This has occurred because of the personality and behavioral profile accompanying Tourette's. Researchers have found that using stimulant medications such as Ritalin, commonly prescribed in attention deficit disorder children, may enhance or even worsen the Tourette symptoms.[6]

THE CHRONICALLY ILL AND/OR HANDICAPPED CHILD

Hank and Ellen sought counseling when the stresses of rearing a child with spina bifida began causing severe marital

discord. They told the therapist they felt distant from one another because the time demands of caring for their daughter
left them no energy to devote to their marriage. Finding a sitter
to stay with their child so they could enjoy an evening out was
hard because of the child's disability. Also, Hank said he felt
excluded from the relationship his wife and disabled daughter
had, since his wife was more intensely involved in meeting her
physical needs than he.

Hank and Ellen are an example of how the presence of a
childhood disability or chronic illness can greatly strain the
child's development and the family itself. Such children not only
are limited in their functioning, but they also face emotional
and behavioral symptoms as a result of the illness or disability.

Family members face similar problems. They must develop
exceptional resources for coping with related stresses. Parents
must work the demands of caring for a disabled child into their
busy family routines without overly disrupting their personal
and vocational lives; they also must learn how to meet other
family members' needs. In addition, the family and child must
cope with the personal grief they feel and the negative attitudes
they encounter on the part of others. They must face the fact
that the child will have limited future opportunities because of
his or her disability.

The child with a chronic illness faces a life of constant struggle and frequent impediments in the process of developing a
healthy self-esteem. For instance, children with asthma must
learn to cope with limits on their physical activities for fear an
asthma attack will occur. Also, many children with asthma have
frightening fears of death when they find themselves unable to
breathe.

Children with epilepsy often become angry and frustrated
about the unpredictable loss of control that occurs during a
seizure episode. They also become angry at being dependent on
medication.

The child with diabetes mellitus may need a shot of insulin
daily or several times daily. This child also must practice rather
rigid diet restrictions while watching his or her peers eat as they
please. The child with cystic fibrosis suffers through multiple

hospitalizations, only to realize that this chronic disease will shorten his or her life.

Children with cancer must endure painful, often body-changing radiation and chemotherapy treatments. Those with chronic kidney disease must depend on dialysis machines for life, and those with chronic heart disease have limited activities in life because of their condition. These and other chronic illnesses present major problems to the child in the process of growing up.

Besides facing the issues of limited physical activities, the child faces frequent blocks to his or her efforts to pursue autonomy and relationships inside and outside the family.

The child's family not only faces the threat of chronic illness and death but also must handle the financial burden the disease brings and the feelings of anger and guilt of family members about having a child with a chronic illness. These families are at risk for serious marital discord. Siblings face depressive and even acting-out behaviors.

The presence of a chronically ill child even affects the parents' child-rearing practices. Sometimes the child faces abuse and neglect; sometimes parents overprotect such a child. For chronically ill children to learn to cope independently, their parents must develop unusual fortitude and must allow the children to encounter more than the usual amount of pain and failure in everyday life.

Furthermore, unhealthy patterns of relationships can develop within the family of such children. As with Hank and Ellen and their spina bifida daughter, the primary caretaker—usually the mother—and the handicapped or chronically ill child develop an exclusive relationship within the family. This is often at the expense of the father and siblings. Other family members may feel they are relegated to the periphery of family life.

How much the disease affects the child psychologically depends on various factors: (1) whether the condition is visible or nonvisible, (2) how restricted the child's activities are, (3) age and onset of the disease, and (4) severity of the illness.

As each of these factors increases, the risk for psychosocial disturbance also seems to increase. The therapist of the child or adolescent involved has a unique opportunity to enhance the quality of life not only for the child but also for the family.

The following are some recommendations for the therapist:

1. Encourage the family and child to seek high-quality medical care. This care should include careful education of the child and family as to the disease process and the treatment process.

2. Support the growing child as he or she faces the issues of impaired autonomy, impaired interpersonal relationships, chronic depression, feelings of helplessness, and chronic feelings of anger and resentment over having this chronic illness.

3. Help the family seek the support of other families familiar with and empathic to chronic illness and its effect on the family.

4. Offer substantial support and courage for the child and the family as they face crises.

5. Direct the family toward specific support groups for families with children experiencing various chronic illnesses or disabilities. These support groups are most often present in the large medical centers, which tend to be the places where parents of these children seek medical treatment.[7]

CHAPTER FIFTEEN

THE CHILD WITH ATTENTION DEFICIT DISORDER

BRENT'S PARENTS SOUGHT COUNSELING after Brent's teacher complained that the eight-year-old youngster daydreamed in class and consistently blurted out while other students worked. The teacher said she had corrected him for the same misbehaviors repeatedly without any noticeable improvement. Other adults who worked with Brent reported the same type of behavior. The boy's parents felt he was being tagged as a problem in his Sunday school class also, and in his scouting group as well. One teacher called him lazy, while another said he had a bad attitude.

Brent later was diagnosed as having attention deficit disorder (ADD), a syndrome accounting for a large percentage of children with behavior and school problems. These children experience incredible frustration in day-to-day life as they attempt to properly perform in school and to rescue their plummeting self-esteem. Similarly, the parents and other family members become frustrated and profoundly discouraged as they try to help these children overcome the difficulties this disorder brings the child and the family.

Far too often, ADD children and their families find themselves mired in helpless and hopeless feelings as they struggle to cope with problems they don't understand and cannot seem to control. Statements that are partially true and much misinformation further confuse the picture.

Attention deficit disorder may be the most underdiagnosed—yet also overdiagnosed—problem in children today. Although many, such as Brent, are labeled "lazy," "bad," or having a "bad attitude," when their problem really is attention deficit disorder, a number of other children with problems are labeled as having ADD even though that is not the case. Only a qualified professional (such as a physician, child psychologist, or educational diagnostician) can diagnose this condition after a careful evaluation.

Attention deficit disorder is a relatively new descriptive term for a problem that has gone under many previous names: hyperactivity, minimal brain dysfunction, cerebral dysfunction. The diagnosis "attention deficit disorder" better describes the basic problem—difficulty with concentration and attention span.

COMMON CHARACTERISTICS

Attention deficit disorders come in two varieties: ADD with hyperactivity and ADD without hyperactivity. Both varieties have these characteristics in common:

1. *Poor attention span.* The child does not finish tasks or work, cannot concentrate or stick with activities or stay on a task.

2. *Distractibility.* As in Brent's case, the child daydreams and is distracted by even the slightest noises, even his or her own thoughts. The central nervous system normally filters out

distractions so people can concentrate on the task at hand. Children with attention deficit disorder have trouble doing this.

3. *Impulsivity.* The child consistently acts without thinking (even though the child knows right from wrong and knows the consequences of misbehavior), shifts from one activity to another, frequently blurts out in class, has trouble awaiting his or her turn, and has trouble delaying gratification. The child also has to be corrected for the same misbehaviors over and over, but this does not imply bad character. Paul Wender of the University of Utah College of Medicine says, "There are certainly ADD kids and ADD adults who are nice and sweet people and who aren't aggressive at all."[1]

4. *Poor social sense.* ADD children tend to miss or misread the nonverbal cues necessary to monitor one's own behavior and tend to say and do the wrong things at the wrong time. They seem not to perceive how their behaviors affect people around them; they tend to laugh or talk too loudly or have an intensity of response that is not appropriate, and they are moody.

As a result of these problems, the ADD child senses anger and rejection from others but cannot seem to understand why. Incredible frustration follows, frequently accompanied by clowning behaviors and tumbling self-esteem.

ADD children who also have the component of hyperactivity often are described as fidgety, are unable to stay seated, and are constantly moving.

These signs and symptoms may not be readily apparent when the child is in a one-on-one situation with an adult. On the other hand, the symptoms worsen in less structured situations, such as recess, gym class, music class, or unstructured neighborhood time. Because several components exist in the ADD syndrome, the problem can occur with varying combinations of the components. A careful diagnosis is imperative.

HOW ADD OCCURS

Not all children with problems have ADD. Researchers say 3 to 10 percent of American children have attention deficit disorder. ADD with hyperactivity appears to be more frequent than without hyperactivity. Eight to ten boys for every girl have the disorder. This sex discrepancy has to do with fetal brain development. Because of the natural changes that occur in the male fetal brain, the male brain seems to be more susceptible to the neurological differences leading to the attention deficit disorder.[2]

Regarding genetic predisposition to ADD, Barry Garfinkel, director of child and adolescent psychiatry at the University of Minnesota Medical School, says, "Though the evidence is tentative, there is some support for a genetic predisposition with the familiar pattern resembling depressive spectrum disease."[3] Attention deficit disorder is not primarily an emotional problem. Rather, it is a neurological problem with a biological basis and behavioral manifestation.

Among the many functions of the human brain—particularly of the two cerebral hemispheres—one function is to coordinate, moderate, direct, and integrate all of the input to and output from the brain. Included in these functions is the process of mediating *attention span, impulse control,* and managing all the *sensory stimuli* coming into the brain. The brain carries out this process through an elaborate system of communication between brain cells by means of chemicals called neurotransmitters. These neurotransmitters are used for cells to communicate with each other and, therefore, to coordinate and organize functions and behaviors.

Empirically, we know that children with attention deficit disorders experience some sort of dysfunction with this neurotransmitter system. Probably there is a slight deficit in the production of these neurotransmitters. If the level of the neurotransmitters is lower, the brain has trouble maintaining attention span, screening out sensory distractions, and organizing impulse control. When these functions lack efficiency, the well-known behaviors of the attention deficit disorder are seen.

To date, it is not known how or why this neurotransmitter dysfunction occurs. We do know that most of the time, ADD is not caused by birth injury, definable pregnancy problems, or head injuries after birth. We also know that many children seem to have an inherited tendency toward ADD. In other words, a child with attention deficit disorder often has a parent or other relative with the same problem.

DIET AND ADD

Currently, great interest exists in the relationship between diet and attention deficit disorder. The most well-known researcher in this field, Ben F. Feingold, author of *Why Your Child Is Hyperactive,* concluded that parents should remove artificial colors, many preservatives, and certain salicylates from the child's diet to decrease the attention deficit disorder symptoms.[4] From Dr. Feingold's work have come many diets and cookbooks, and many people follow these scrupulously. Other researchers feel certain vitamin or mineral deficiencies either cause or contribute to ADD symptoms. Still different diets and cookbooks have come from their work. To say the least, many people disagree about how effective these approaches are.

To date, no clear-cut scientific evidence has emerged finding the dietary or megavitamin approach to ADD to be thoroughly effective. However, anyone who has spent time with ADD children knows that excessive sugar intake and some food additives seem to worsen their symptoms.

It is probably best to limit as much as possible the intake of such substances in the child's diet. But to eliminate them entirely is probably not as effective as some would hope and may not even be possible with most children. It is interesting to note that many ADD children seem to have an inordinate craving for sugar products. Therefore, restricting sugar from their diets can be hard at times. However, we do agree that restricting sugar intake is probably in the best interests of all children. Dental experts certainly concur.

Some people believe that allergies cause ADD. Again, to date, no conclusive scientific research exists to document this. However, research is not yet complete in this area. Many drugs that are used to treat allergic symptoms, and even cold symptoms (antihistamines, etc.), tend to adversely affect ADD children. No credible research data supports either treating with megadoses of vitamins or treating with large amounts of trace elements, such as copper, zinc, magnesium, manganese, and chromium.[5]

MEDICATIONS FOR TREATING ADD

With this knowledge in mind, we can begin to understand how medication is used to treat attention deficit disorder. While several medications are available to treat ADD, most of them have the same mode of action—to increase the brain cells' production of neurotransmitters and to make those neurotransmitters more efficient. "Although a massive quantity of accumulated research has demonstrated unequivocally that the majority of hyperactive children respond positively to treatment with psychostimulants, not all do," says Jan Loney of the department of psychiatry and behavioral science of the State University of New York.[6] Medicines used most commonly are:

• *Dexedrine* (generic name dextroamphetamine). This is a stimulant medication. Years ago it was discovered accidentally that this medication actually calmed down children with attention deficit disorder. We believe it works because it actually stimulates the brain cells to produce more normal levels of neurotransmitters. When these levels are reached, the brain can do its job of coordinating, integrating, and calming down input to and output from the brain.

When persons without attention deficit disorder take this medication, they may appear to be agitated, excited, and even hyperactive because, again, their neurotransmitter level is out of balance. Dexedrine is available in regular-dose tablets and in a sustained-release capsule to extend the medication's effect. As with any medication, possible side effects occur, the most common of which are irritability and loss of appetite.

• *Ritalin* (generic name methylphenidate). Ritalin is a medication similar to Dexedrine in its action and effects. It is the most widely used medication for attention deficit disorder because of its specificity and rapid onset of action. Ritalin also comes in regular-dose tablets and in a sustained-release form. Its possible side effects can be similar to those of Dexedrine.

Much discussion has occurred about Ritalin's effect on growth in children. Little if any risk is involved in affecting a child's growth. Nevertheless, a physician should follow closely the child taking Ritalin, monitoring the child's height and weight. Ritalin has a rapid onset of action, but its effect rapidly disappears. The sustained-release form has a longer period of action.

Frequently, children taking Ritalin have "drug vacations" on weekends and during the summer. The decision to cease medication, even temporarily, needs to be made jointly between the physician and the parents. They should take into account all factors, including how the child's behavior off medications will affect the child and others.

• *Cylert* (generic name pemoline). Cylert acts similarly to the stimulants mentioned earlier. Its main advantage is its longer duration of action, requiring only one dose per day. Since Cylert requires a longer time to achieve a therapeutic blood level, two to three weeks may be needed to determine if Cylert will help the child.

• *Tofranil* (generic name imiprimine). While Tofranil is an antidepressant, not a stimulant, it has been used with some success in some children with attention deficit disorder. Tofranil appears to have a positive effect on producing neurotransmitters which control the area of attention span and distractibility.

All the above medications have as their primary therapeutic effect an increase in attention span, which improves task performance. Because the child's concentration span increases, the child can better monitor his or her behavior also.

Other medications also have been used in managing children with attention deficit disorder. Such medications have different modes of action than do those listed earlier. The medications listed below tend to have a tranquilizing effect rather than a stimulating effect on the brain.

1. *Mellaril* (generic name thioridazine) or *Thorazine* (generic name chlorpromazine) or *Haldol* (generic name halopendol). All of these are classified as major tranquilizers and are used only in special situations for the attention deficit disorder child. The stimulant medications above are more specific and more effective in managing the ADD symptoms.

2. *Benadryl* (generic name diphenhydramine). This well-known antihistamine occasionally is used in large doses with

children having attention deficit disorder. Again, the stimulant medications are probably a better form of medication management, except in special cases.

Children should understand as fully as possible why they are taking a medication. Frequently children will say they take medication for hyperactivity because they are "bad," or, conversely, that the medication makes them "good." The parent should tell the child that he or she has trouble concentrating, which frequently leads to trouble completing school work and other tasks. Failing to complete these tasks can lead to negative consequences. The child should know that the medication will help increase the attention span and concentration.

For the child who also has trouble with impulse control, the parent should explain that the medication helps the child control his or her behavior. The parent should stress that the medicine will not *control* behavior, but that it will help the child be more in control.

The child must understand that the medicine is not magic or a "cure-all." Even when the child is on the medicine, he or she will continue to have good and bad days, both with behavior and with school performance.

The parent should use the medicine just as the physician prescribes it. To use the medication any other way will not give it a fair chance to have the desired effect.

Younger children usually comply with taking medications, but they will start to resist as they become older. This is especially true for the older child who has to take a midday dose at school. The child sometimes become embarrassed and refuses to go for the dose.

Medication must not become an issue in a power struggle. Parents need to consistently explain the benefits of the medication while expressing empathy for the child who resents having to take medication. To avoid parent-child power struggles over the medication, the child and physician probably should have an honest discussion about the matter.

Parents sometimes wonder whether the use of this medication will lead to later drug abuse. After extensive experience and a review of clinical studies, no findings indicate that taking any medication for control of ADD causes drug abuse in the future.

We do know, however, that ADD, because of its inherent difficulty with impulse control and its recurrent difficulty with dwindling self-esteem, puts children and teen-agers at increased risk for drug abuse later in life. This is a well-documented fact. Rachel Gittleman's study, published in the *Archives of General Psychiatry*, followed children from about age eleven until their late teens and early twenties. It found that children with ADD were at twice the risk for alcohol and substance abuse.[7]

When is the appropriate time to stop ADD medication? We believe every child needs an occasional trial period off medication to verify the medicine's effectiveness and the need to continue it. As a child becomes older, these trials off medicine will become more important. The parent, patients, and doctor must weigh heavily the pluses and minuses of being on or off the medication before they make a decision.

MANAGING THE ADD CHILD AT HOME

Children with ADD usually are fun and loving people to be around. However, an incredible amount of hurt and frustration can relate to their behavior problems. Often, parents have made many well-intentioned efforts to help the child adjust his or her behavior so that the child can find the approval and acceptance he or she desperately needs. These well-intentioned efforts often end with parents who are frustrated and children who wish to please parents, peers, and other adults but who find themselves puzzled over their inability to monitor their behaviors without help.

The same discipline guidelines that apply to all children apply to the ADD child. However, some special guidelines for the ADD child do exist. Parents should try to prevent behavior problems, because once the ADD child is in trouble, frequently his or her behavior will further deteriorate.

A number of difficulties may be prevented by the parents' willingness to truly understand the ADD child. Parents should remember that ADD is a physical disability. While the disability often is a subtle one, it does make the child different from other children in such areas as finishing tasks, controlling impulses, and monitoring one's own behavior. To prevent problems, the parent will need to help the child organize tasks into smaller segments. Preventing problems for the ADD child requires that the parents consistently exercise much patience, wisdom, and persistence.

Parents should keep to a consistent daily schedule to help prevent problems. Disorganized, unstructured situations as well as frequent changes in the family routine are sure to increase inappropriate behaviors in the ADD child. It helps to have a daily schedule as well as daily chores written out and easily accessible to the child because this provides structure and clear expectations. Such structure contributes to success, which will pay important dividends in terms of a child's healthy self-esteem.

Parents should make every effort to guard the child's self-esteem. Because of the nature of their disorder, these children are prone to frequent criticism, failure, and even rejection. This especially damages their self-esteem because they do not fully understand how they get themselves into such negative situations.

When the ADD child's self-esteem is dwindling, he or she frequently turns to inappropriate behaviors—clowning, explosive outbursts, or a "chip-on-the-shoulder" attitude. Generally, the parent should respond by being firm and fair and should point the child to more appropriate behavior. Empathy for the child is important, but so is the commitment to redirecting the child to appropriate expectations. Parents will find that consistency and patience will pay off immensely.

Parents should remember that ADD is a biological and physical problem. Difficulty with attention span, impulse control, and fidgetiness stems from biological problems and are not willful misbehaviors. Parents should not punish a child for something he or she cannot control without help, but should keep their expectations appropriate for the child. ADD is a chronic condition. While symptoms will improve with age, parents should remember that the symptoms will not stop in a matter of a year or two, let alone a week or two.

The course of the attention deficit disorder can vary. Plateaus, peaks, and valleys in behavior can occur. Parents should remember that all children, especially children with ADD, require not only negative consequences but also the chance for positive consequences that will build new, more appropriate behaviors. Negative consequences only diminish inappropriate behaviors; they do not give an option for change. Parents also should remember that materialistic positive consequences—such as money or toys—occasionally may be appropriate, but social-reward consequences—rewarding experiences with the family or family members—are the most important tools in establishing appropriate behaviors.

WAYS TO EXTINGUISH NEGATIVE BEHAVIOR

The parent may need some hints for extinguishing negative behaviors. In sessions with the parent, the counselor can share from this list of advisory tips:

1. *Remember that ADD children are impulsive.* Parents, finding themselves responding to the same misbehaviors over and over again, should be consistent and patient in such matters.

2. *Administer immediate consequences.* To help the ADD child extinguish negative behaviors, this is important.

3. *Clearly identify the limits and consequences.*

4. *Give one warning when disobedience occurs.* If it continues, a firm and consistent follow-through of consequences is necessary.

5. *Help the child to understand that behavior and consequences are the child's choice.* While ADD is a biological and physical disorder, children still must learn that their behavior and its consequences are their choice. To do this the parent must provide structure—that is, clear expectations and consequences.

6. *Identify or label behaviors specifically.* Don't just call the child or the behavior "bad," but identify the behaviors that are inappropriate. For example, say, "what you did was rude" or "what you did was hurtful." Then specifically link the inappropriate behavior to the consequence, such as, "because what you did was rude, this is what will happen."

7. *Have a repertoire of consequences.* Many parents of ADD

children find spanking these children creates even more problems and that other types of consequences sometimes are necessary. Alternate consequences could include loss of privileges and being isolated in a room for a brief period of time.

8. *Make sure the child has opportunities to make restitution for inappropriate behavior.* Even if it is only partial restitution, it is important that all children not only experience negative consequences for misbehavior but also have chances to make restitution for their misdeeds.

9. *Be careful not to punish for "bad attitude."* Punish for misbehaviors resulting from a bad attitude. A parent cannot control a child's thoughts and attitudes, but the parent can control the behavior that results from bad attitudes.

10. *Intervene early in a misbehavior situation.* Parents should intervene early and stay in control, not allowing anger to take control. When the child's anger is *out of control,* the child should know the parent will choose to be *in control.*

As already mentioned, negative consequences only temporarily extinguish inappropriate behaviors. It is a positive consequence that builds new and appropriate behavior. With that in mind, here are some hints parents can use for building acceptable behaviors:

1. Consistently recognize and reward appropriate behaviors—even if they are small—in the child. When a parent recognizes and approves appropriate behaviors, it means more to the child than does any toy or other materialistic object. Parents may need to do this over and over again, but it is well worth the effort.

2. Choose only a few behaviors at a time to build into the child. Make sure a good chance for success exists for building these behaviors. Starting small ensures that success will breed more success.

3. Clearly identify the tasks or behaviors expected. If the child chooses these behaviors, identify them with positive consequences.

4. The parent may need to help the ADD child organize himself or herself to achieve success. Using specific time limits and written lists frequently helps. Parents also need to monitor the task to help ensure success.

5. Make sure the parent has the child's full attention when presenting instructions. Remember, ADD children can be very inattentive. The parent may need to use several ways to communicate to the child. For instance, the parent may need to first say, "Listen to me," when talking to the child. Touching the child with a hand on his or her shoulder often helps. The parent also may need to use hand gestures or written lists to visually reinforce the instructions.

Parents should be confident in themselves as parents and in the position of authority God has given them as parents. They should not allow fear of their child's unhappiness to lead them to avoid confrontations with the child. They should stay in control and always have foremost in their minds what is in the child's best interest.

Counselors should remind parents that they should do whatever is necessary to protect the family relationships, since those relationships are absolutely essential to the child's success and happiness as an adult. Fortunately, God has created children in a way that what is in the child's best interest also is in the family's best interest, and vice versa.

MANAGING THE ADD CHILD AT SCHOOL

Ted, seven, an ADD child, started school in an open-concept classroom and was seated in the back row of desks. After only a few days, Ted began leaving his seat and roaming throughout the entire first-grade area. The slightest noise from the neighboring classroom kept Ted preoccupied, preventing his being attentive to his teacher. Ted's behavior improved tremendously when his teacher switched him to a contained classroom and positioned him on the front row near the teacher's desk.

Managing the ADD child in a school setting requires teachers to understand thoroughly the attention deficit disorder. Teachers must realize that these children have special needs, since their behaviors associated with ADD will be chronic. Also, they will need to know that ADD children have trouble not only with attention span but also in relating to peers.

As Ted's teacher learned, the ADD child performs best in a structured classroom where as few distractions as possible occur. Usually, the child needs to sit in a desk near the teacher.

The ADD child will do best with a teacher who is structured and firm—but not rigid—and who develops a personal, trusting relationship with the child. Angry, confronting episodes with the ADD child will worsen behaviors as well as destroy his or her self-esteem.

Constructive criticism, firm limits, and positive personal relationships will do wonders for the ADD child. He or she may be viewed as the "class clown," as explosive, or as having a chip on his or her shoulder. However, ADD children use all these behaviors to protect their fragile self-esteem.

Cooperation between the school and home of an ADD child is imperative. Both parents and school must understand the ADD child so that appropriate expectations can be established.

Managing the Child at Other Places

All information discussed under "home" and "school" is important for other places where the child is involved. An additional word here is needed, however. Often, adults in church, youth groups, scouting, athletic programs, and other such organizations find it easy to be angry with and critical of children with attention deficit disorder. Adults in these organizations play a major role in helping the ADD child build appropriate behaviors and a healthy self-esteem, but they can only do this if they fully understand how best to handle the ADD child. They, too, must focus on firmness and consistency. An adult's angry, resentful approach most surely will worsen the problems of the ADD child.

Because they get criticized by those who lack an understanding of the problems of ADD children, parents of these children can be helped by being part of support groups. It helps to know that other parents face the same problems, and it also helps to share ideas and experiences with people in similar dilemmas.

CHAPTER SIXTEEN

LEARNING DISABILITIES

JONATHAN'S MOTHER NEEDED HIM to help her with chores. She asked him to empty the wastebaskets and to restack the family's videocassette tapes neatly on the shelves in the study.

An hour later, however, Mom found that Jonathan, five, had emptied only the study wastebasket and was seated in front of the television watching a video, with the rest of the work unfinished.

Normally, a parent would punish Jonathan for not following her instructions, for "goofing off" on the job. But Jonathan has a learning disability, an auditory perceptual problem allowing him to hear only fragments of his mother's verbal instruction to him. As a result, he became confused and thought Mom asked him to empty the study wastebasket and watch a video afterward.

Cases such as this can cause extreme stress for children, parents, teachers, and any caregiver uninformed about learning disabilities. The term *learning disabilities* refers to a large group of disorders—disorders that show up when children have trouble acquiring and using their listening, speaking, reading, writing, reasoning, or mathematical abilities. Experts widely assume that these disorders stem from central nervous system dysfunction.

While learning disabilities may occur simultaneously *with* environmental stresses or other emotional disorders or handicapping conditions (for example, sensory impairment or mental retardation), it is widely assumed that learning disabilities do not result *from* these factors. They occur even when children have normal or above-normal general intelligence. Problems lie generally in the areas of processing sensory input or in producing academic output. In short, these children have normal to above-normal intelligence but have trouble performing for one reason or another in the classroom.

It is difficult to estimate how prevalent learning disabilities are, because no one agrees on a clear definition of them. However, experts generally agree that about 10 percent of all school-aged children have some form of learning disability.

Boys with learning disabilities seem to outnumber girls at a ratio of two to one. Once again, this is thought to result from the differences in how the male brain develops in utero compared to the female brain.

Therapeutic intervention with learning-disabled children must be based on assessing the total child in his or her environment. This is important because learning disabilities are not just school problems. They interfere with all aspects of the child's life, including psychosocial development, peer interactions, and family interactions. A high percentage of learning-disabled children have problems with attention deficit disorder. A great number of such children also develop secondary emotional, social, and family problems.

CATEGORIES OF LEARNING DISABILITIES

Although descriptions and diagnoses vary widely, learning disabilities fall into the following general categories:

1. *Difficulties with processing sensory input.* This category comprises a group of perceptual problems and may involve any of the five senses. The two dysfunctions most commonly found are visual- and auditory-perceptual disabilities. Children with a visual-perceptual disability may have trouble organizing visual input, particularly in relationship to position in space.

When faced with a symbol, particularly a letter of the alphabet or a word, they may reverse it or transpose it. Furthermore, they have difficulty with spatial relationships. They confuse right and left and otherwise lose their bearings in space.

Another aspect of this type of learning disability is a problem in distinguishing the significant elements of a visual situation from its background. For example, when Jimmy takes a test in school, he may be asked to look at a drawing and tell how many more chickens than cows are in the picture. However, if Jimmy has this type of learning disability, he may be unable to distinguish the animals from the actual background in the drawing. Therefore, he is unable to answer the question correctly, even though he may know his math facts well.

2. *Auditory perceptual problems.* As mentioned earlier in the incident with young Jonathan, children with this type of learning disability find it hard to distinguish subtle differences in sound. Therefore, they may misunderstand or misperceive or even miss much auditory input. These children have trouble processing sound as quickly as ordinary speech requires. Therefore, the auditory lag causes them to miss part of what they hear.

This creates obvious difficulties in a classroom or anywhere when the child receives verbal instructions. Verbal communication often confuses these children, and they do not follow through to obey the communication.

3. *Difficulties with integrating information after the brain has perceived it.* The child may incorrectly sequence information as a result of this disorder. If the teacher tells such children to sharpen their pencils, work their math problems, and then turn them in, they may perform these tasks out of order. They may have much trouble inferring abstract meaning from literal sensory input. A child such as this would have difficulty with abstract problems like, "Cold is to winter as _____ (hot) is to summer."

4. *Difficulty with memory.* The child perceives and integrates information but has trouble accessing this information in the memory areas of the brain. In certain children, this disability involves only short-term memory—that is, memory retained only as long as one attends to the information at hand. For others, however, the trouble is with long-term memory, or recalling information that has been permanently stored.

5. *Output disabilities.* This involves the process of getting information from the brain. It may include trouble in expressing oneself in words, by means of language, or through muscle activity or motor output. Language disabilities usually involve difficulty with communicating one's thoughts and feelings with words.

Trouble also may occur in the area of gross or fine motor performance. Gross motor difficulty might cause the child to be clumsy or to have trouble with large motor skills such as skating, riding a bike, or running. Fine motor disabilities may cause the child to have trouble organizing combinations of small muscles to work together.

In school, this is most commonly noted in the areas of written language. Many children have this particular type of learning disability, in which they have no difficulty with sensory input and memory, but have a great deal of trouble putting into writing what they have learned or have created in their minds.

Obviously, this causes much frustration in the classroom, particularly as the child becomes older and teachers evaluate most of the child's performance by means of written language. As children with this writing disability—frequently called dysgraphia—progress through the school grades, they become increasingly frustrated with written work. They soon would rather face criticism for not doing their work than face the frustration of trying to express themselves in written language.

The presence of learning disabilities in a child creates much frustration for that child. These children sense themselves as being different from their peers, particularly in the classroom. They also have this perception in social and family settings. They may have trouble following instructions, understanding complex social situations, and expressing themselves.

Becoming frustrated with their repeated failures, they have trouble coping with situations. As a result, they often experience social and emotional problems.

If children with learning disabilities have continual difficulties and frustration and failure interacting with the outside world, they are at high risk for difficulties with the process of separation and individuation. It is clear, then, that early diagnosis and effective intervention and treatment are important in children with learning disabilities.

DIAGNOSING LEARNING DISABILITIES

Specifically diagnosing learning disabilities may be difficult. Because many experts still disagree on their exact definition, various professionals will differ on the correct way to diagnose and evaluate them.

Generally, however, experts recognize that specific psycho-educational testing is necessary. The most frequently used tests include the Wide Range Achievement Test, the Wechsler Intelligence Scale for Children-Revised, the Woodcock-Johnson Battery, and the Detroit Test.

In general, these testing instruments look for variations in different areas of cognitive abilities. To diagnose the learning disability, one either must find a significant variation in the different subtest of cognitive skills or find a significant discrepancy between the child's tested aptitude and the actual academic performance in the classroom.

Evaluating a child for learning disabilities also must include a careful neurological examination by a physician and a careful assessment of the child's total growth and physical development. This is necessary to pick up the other significant factors often accompanying learning disabilities.

TREATING LEARNING DISABILITIES

Treating learning disabilities requires a broad-based approach to the child and his or her family. The treatment program may use any or all of the following five components.

1. *School-based programs.* Once a child has been tested and diagnosed as having learning disabilities, most local school

systems offer special educational help for him or her. The best school program is the one offering what the child needs academically with the fewest environmental restrictions.

For the younger child, the focus will be on remedial approaches designed to minimize or overcome specific disabilities. Grade-expected skills will be taught through the use of individual learning strengths. These capitalize on the child's strengths while trying to overcome the child's specific learning disabilities.

Specifically, the child learns new skills through multisensory type approaches. For instance, the child may learn the alphabet not only through visual means but also through tactile means—touching plastic figures representing each letter of the alphabet.

Qualified professionals must teach these programs. The child may have only one to two hours a day in this specialized program or may spend the entire school day in a self-contained classroom where teachers use these techniques to educate the child.

The goal is to expedite the child's learning progress and to reinstate the child in regular education classes as soon as he or she is ready.

Recently, numerous private schools have been established for children with learning disabilities. These schools offer well-balanced, full academic programs with extracurricular activities approximating the regular public school experience for the child who has learning disabilities. As the child ages, special education needs may be directed more toward prevocational and vocational training.

2. *Family counseling.* The counselor's first job is to educate the parents about their son's or daughter's learning disabilities. The counselor should explain how these disabilities affect not only school performance but also family and peer interactions. The family should learn to maximize the child's learning strengths. They need to know their child's intellectual potential, level of academic performance, and why he or she is underachieving.

Parents need to learn strategies to help the child feel as normal and as successful as possible, both in the family and with peers.

Educators recommend teaching children to break down tasks into smaller portions so that successful completion is possible. Others teach alternative communication skills using both visual and auditory techniques so the children clearly understand instructions. Others recommend supervising them as they complete their tasks so they do not become distracted or confused in the process of completing this work.

Most of all, the child must learn that the parents value him or her despite the learning disabilities. However, parents must avoid overprotecting the child.

3. *Individual therapy and behavior interventions.* The therapist must be sure the proper educational program is in effect for the child. The therapist must be sure the parents understand the child's learning disabilities. After this, the therapist should spend time with the individual child explaining the child's strengths and weaknesses. The therapist should tell the child that he or she is a valuable member of the family, the school, and the community.

Frequently, children need some individual therapy time to work through interpersonal and intrapsychic conflicts. Parent and therapist must remember that children with learning disabilities will exhibit those same disabilities in counseling as they do in the school and in the family. Therefore, the counselor must be willing to be patient and exercise a wide variety of intervention skills using alternative sensory inputs. He or she will want to be sensitive to the child's problem with disorganization or memory or other learning problems.

Many times their intermittent contact with the therapist is a lifeline for children with learning disabilities as they grow up.

4. *Medication therapy.* If a child with learning disabilities also has an attention deficit disorder—as many as 40 percent of them do[1]—then medication may well be of help. Such medication decreases distractibility and increases attention span. It may even improve some forms of fine motor difficulties. However, medication never treats the underlying learning disabilities. Educational therapy is still essential.

5. *More controversial therapies.* Frequently, opthalmologists and optometrists perform eye evaluations on children

with learning disabilities. Certainly, such a child should have primary visual problems ruled out.

Optometrists also frequently think they can treat the primary learning disabilities by using eye exercises. This is a controversial form of treatment. Many organizations have studied it at length. The American Academy of Pediatrics and the American Academy of Opthalmology have issued a joint statement criticizing these exercises as treatment for the primary causes of learning disabilities. They strongly emphasize the need for a multidisciplinary approach to the treatment. No single professional can ever evaluate or treat the whole child with learning disabilities.[2]

Vestibular dysfunction therapy is a new form of therapy advanced by Levinson.[3] The role of the vestibular system in higher cortical function, such as learning, is not yet clearly understood. Recent studies find no evidence supporting either the vestibular theories of learning disabilities or the proposed treatment approaches.

CHAPTER SEVENTEEN

THE SPIRITUAL TRAINING
OF THE CHILD

A CLASS OF TWENTY-THREE FIRST GRADERS sat so still they hardly blinked an eyelash during a thirty-minute movie. Afterward, a visiting parent commented to her daughter, "I don't think I've ever seen a group of children be so quiet." Her child replied, "We have to, Mommy, or the teacher will make us come back to the classroom and stay in during recess." The child sat motionless to avoid the teacher's wrath.

Such cooperation results from what those who study the moral and spiritual development of children would call "Stage 1" understanding. Children appear to go through a series of well-defined stages of understanding of spiritual and ethical matters. In the grade-school years, the child especially focuses on what constitutes "doing right versus doing wrong."

Among the leading researchers in this area are Dan Motet and the late Lawrence Kohlberg. Kohlberg, a researcher in child development, has defined the six stages of spiritual development and Motet has developed the idea further.

Motet points out that Kohlberg's six stages of development in the child rather closely follow the progressive stages God used in "training" the children of Israel from a position of slavery to being the free-standing nation of Israel and "God's own people." Motet says:

> Kohlberg's approach is analogous to what we find in Scripture, where we can follow God's work to raise human moral judgment through the six stages. The events that started with Exodus are a good example.[1]

Kohlberg has said children progress through six stages of moral development:

Stage 1—*The Punishment-Obedience Orientation.* In this stage, as with the first grader in the introductory example, the child essentially acts in order to avoid punishment and out of a sense of deference to authority or power.

In Stage 1 in the Bible, we can see that the nation Israel in Exodus 14:31 accepted Moses' leadership because they feared the Lord. The relationship there between God and Israel represented their need to comply with strict absolutes. The children of Israel had been in the bondage of slavery for four hundred years, heeding the beckoning call of hedonistic Egypt. As a result, they were capable only of the punishment-avoiding and deference-to-power type of relationship found in Stage 1.

Stage 2—*The Instrument-Relativist Orientation.* In this stage, the child begins to see right actions and good conduct as those behaviors which do more than simply avoid punishment. They also see these behaviors as serving to meet one's own need and the needs of others. A sense of reciprocity occurs where right human relationships take on a sense of fairness and justice. A true sense of cooperation develops here.

In Stage 2, the child in the above example remains quiet in the movie because he doesn't want to disturb his neighbor and also because he knows Freddy will be kinder to him on the playground if he doesn't bug Freddy during the video.

Motet points out that in Exodus 16:2–3, we see that motivation out of deference to power is replaced by more of a bartering mentality, in which the relative pluses and minuses of a decision are weighed.

Israel's people are upset about a lack of food, and they vacillate between the unknown future and a willingness to sacrifice freedom, return to Egypt, and there have plentiful food. In Stage 2, children begin to weigh the relative merits of decisions, one against the other. This is based not only on the concept of punishment but also on the relative benefits of either course they could take.

Stage 3—*The Interpersonal Concordance,* or "Good Boy-Nice Girl" Orientation. In this stage, the child begins genuinely longing for others' approval.

The child whispers the right answer to her fellow student during a test because the child wants to be popular. Or, sometimes, the child can do the right thing in order to please others. She can go back through the cafeteria line for more butter patties, not necessarily because she wants to serve others but because she hopes her classmates will elect her "Student of the Week."

Aaron is caught up in this dilemma when he gives in to Israel's requests and builds them a golden calf (Exodus 32). This ends up being a disastrous mistake, but to Aaron it seemed "good behavior" in the immediate sense because it pleased others.

Stage 4—*The Law-and-Order Orientation.* In this stage of development, the philosophical foundation stones of the child's moral development are strengthened as certain immutable principles are inculcated into the child's conscience.

The child obeys the classroom rules because he or she knows they are right and good. No longer does the child operate solely out of fear of authority, as in Stage 1, but because he or she can internalize why the classroom rules are good for everyone.

We see God's work with Israel in something of a Stage 4 fashion as God gives the Ten Commandments to Moses. This forms the foundation which standardizes the moral absolutes between God and Israel (Exodus 20:1–17).

Motet makes the interesting observation that the Pharisees in the New Testament appeared to be fixated in Stage 4. Jesus often was embroiled in controversy with the Pharisees and wanted them to appreciate a more mature and accurate relationship with God. In Stage 5, we will see how Jesus made certain commandments flexible in order to serve the truer high purpose of the commandments' original intent.

Stage 5—*The Social-Contract Orientation* with Utilitarian Overtones. In this phase, the bedrock of personal rights and agreed-upon standards becomes fixed in the child's own mind as well as in the social fabric of relationships in which he or she engages.

However, the concept of flexibility begins to enter here. We see Jesus, in Matthew 12:1–14, attempting to show the Pharisees how flexibility relates to God's commands. In that passage, Jesus explains that even though the Sabbath is important to God, the Sabbath was made for man and not man for the Sabbath.

During the adolescent years, young persons begin to exercise Stage 5 decision-making skills, modifying and yet not setting aside proven standards of conduct from their earlier years.

Adolescents who have not been allowed to develop a progressively more complex code of conduct, but who have had others' values forced down their throats, will, at this point, often react against much of their moral teachings. Sometimes they will totally reverse their conduct and turn against the principles of parents and church. Rather than modifying and making more flexible their code of ethics, these young people repudiate their previous upbringing.

In later years, these young people may return to a more normative baseline of conduct, often quite similar to that of their parents. But the tragedy of this kind of absolute, heartbreaking rejection of the parents' value system is that it is not always necessary.

Stage 6—*The Universal-Ethical-Principle Orientation.* In this stage, the person is guided by conscience and, as the Scriptures teach, the "law of liberty," with ethical principles that now emanate from the personal depths of an individual's walk with God.

We see this in Moses' life during his latter years. He pled

with God for his people's well-being and unselfishly risked his own future for them. Eventually people called him "the friend of God."

The individual develops an appreciation for God's majesty, the dignity of human beings, and the universal principles of justice, love, and applicability of the Christian faith. This stage is entered in later adolescence and early adulthood.

An example of this Stage 6 orientation is the young person who receives too much change when she buys eyeshadow at the department store and alerts the clerk to the mistake. The young person can internalize what God's Word teaches about cheating and stealing. She also knows that the clerk will be unable to balance her cash at the end of the day if she keeps the money. The young person is able to apply her Christian faith and her understanding of love for other human beings in such a situation.

As counselors seek to help the parents of grade-school-age children, they will find children working through Stage 3 and developing firm Stage 4 personal codes of conduct. Such children will seek to learn how decisions impact their codes of conduct and just what the flexibility to make decisions means in terms of freedom, responsibilities, and consequences.

The following grid (Figure 17–1) is a simple device that we have used to counsel parents. In this, we see the four "quadrants" grade-school children use in deliberating over decisions they make.

Activities falling in Quadrant 1 are easy for the young person to deal with since they are enjoyable and morally right. They bring pleasurable rewards and coincide with the child's sense of conscience.

Items in Quadrant 2 require self-discipline. These activities are right to do, but they are not necessarily enjoyable. For example, performing an unselfish act of service to others with little immediate personal pleasure falls into this category. An example would be a child who spends a Saturday helping repair the crumbling front porch of an elderly neighbor.

Noted psychologist David Elkind says, "We need to restore our sense of community and to rediscover the truth that cooperation can be as healthy and as important as competition."[2]

	The Activity is *ENJOYABLE*	The Activity is *NOT ENJOYABLE*
The Activity is RIGHT TO DO	1	2
The Activity is NOT RIGHT TO DO	3	4

Figure 17–1
Decision-Making Grid

Decisions that require action in Quadrant 2 may not be competitive, exciting, or particularly pleasurable. But they do build character.

Activities in Quadrant 3 require self-control. These activities are not right morally, yet they offer the prospect of immediate pleasurable reward. The temptation to steal an attractive hair bow when little chance of being caught exists would be a Quadrant 3 decision dilemma.

Activities involving Quadrant 4 also are relatively easy to decide because they are not right nor are they enjoyable. For example, children who have no interest in bullying other children and who also feel bullying is wrong would have little trouble avoiding a physical altercation where they are in control.

As grade-school children push forward to develop moral absolutes for themselves, skills in decision making and good parental assistance are indispensable to them. This is especially true in the love-and-service decisions of Quadrant 2 and the personal-purity and moral-uprightness decisions of Quadrant 3. The counselor will have as a goal that grade-school children will see their parents demonstrating good decision making. Parents whose decisions are sound practically and biblically help strengthen the children's spiritual development.

The Christian counselor has a unique opportunity to support

and strengthen the spiritual growth of the child by offering to that child a caring and compassionate relationship in which problems can be addressed and answers found. This counselor can also help the family focus on the priorities necessary for the child's spiritual growth by helping parents to:

1. Promote a family in which relationships are the top priority. Nothing is more important than relationships. The unconditional love of God is best modeled in the family where there is a healthy marriage and healthy parent-child relationships. A child's spiritual growth is strongly encouraged when the parents' marriage is healthy. A Christian counselor must encourage healthy marriages.

2. Recognize that God has not called parents to be perfect, but to love their children—and raise them in the Lord. A parent's recognition of his or her own imperfections actually facilitates the introduction of the Perfect Heavenly Father above.

3. Commit to teaching a healthy self-esteem that includes the knowledge that we are created in God's image, that we are fallen (sinners) but not worthless, and that we are supremely and sacrifically loved by the Heavenly Father. These factors are the key to a healthy self-esteem as opposed to self-centeredness. A healthy self-esteem is essential to a child's spiritual growth.

4. Recognize that our worth is based not in what we do, but who we are and whose we are. Perfectionism is a "works" salvation doctrine and stifles spiritual growth.

5. Acknowledge that the Bible is God's Word. The Bible is useful every day. The guidelines contained therein are given by a God who loves us and knows us better than we will ever know ourselves. Therefore, his guidelines are given in *our best interest.* Similarly, the Bible is God's message of love to us. Its words and stories are meant to convey his love for us. Read it daily, not out of duty, but out of excitement in hearing from God.

6. Make a priority of the parents' own spiritual growth. When parents make spiritual growth an exciting part of every day, children will seek their own spiritual growth.

The Christian counselor has an exciting opportunity to encourage all these goals and, in so doing, bring an excitement to the children he or she counsels.

NOTES

Chapter 1 Winning the Child-Rearing Contest

1. Robert Trotter, "Three Heads Are Better Than One, A Profile on Robert I. Sternberg, Ph.D.," *Psychology Today,* August 1986, 56–62.

2. *Developmental Neuropsychiatry,* Michael Rutter, ed. (New York: The Guilford Press, 1983), 164–68.

3. Ross Campbell, *How to Really Love Your Child* (Wheaton, Ill.: Victor Books, 1977).

Chapter 2 Needs of the Young Child

1. Clarence J. Rowe, *An Outline of Psychiatry,* 9th ed. (Dubuque: William C. Brown Publishers, 1989), 25–26.

2. "Infants Keep Imitation in Mind," *Science News,* 134 (23 July 1988), 62.

3. "Childhood Gender-Identity Disorder Linked to Homosexuality," *Convention Reporter Newsletter,* a report on the 141st annual meeting, American Psychiatric Association, vol. 18, no. 15, June 1988.

Chapter 3 Options of the Young Child

1. Nancy Rubin, "Your Child's Temperament, Easy, Difficult or Slow-to-Warm-Up," *Parents*, September 1987, 94–98, 224–27.
2. Stanley K. Turecki and Leslie Tonner, *The Difficult Child* (New York: Bantam Books, 1987).
3. David Elkind and Irving Weiner, *Development of the Child* (New York: John Wiley and Sons, 1978), 355.
4. Ibid.
5. Ibid.
6. Ross Campbell, *How to Really Love Your Child* (Wheaton, Ill.: Victor Books, 1977), 120, 121.

Chapter 4 Ways for Change with the Young Child

1. Martin Goldberg, "Parental Sabotage," *Medical Aspects of Human Sexuality*, February 1988, 34–41.
2. Richard Camer, "Soft Words Speak Louder with Kids," *Psychology Today*, December 1983, 14.
3. Wilson Wayne Grant, *The Caring Father* (Nashville: Broadman, 1983).
4. Gordon MacDonald, *The Effective Father* (Wheaton, Ill.: Tyndale House, 1977).
5. Michael Lamb, "Will the Real New Father Please Stand Up?" *Parents*, June 1987, 77–80.
6. Ibid.
7. John Reinhart, "Should Parents Try to Be 'Pals' to Their Children?" *Medical Aspects of Human Sexuality*, vol. 17, no. 6 (June 1986), 67.

Chapter 5 More Ways for Change with the Young Child

1. *Comprehensive Study of Adult Development, 1970–1988*, George E. Vaillant, dir./ed., Dartmouth Medical School, Department of Psychiatry, Hanover, New Hampshire.
2. Ibid.
3. Sally Valente Kiester and Edwin Kiester, Jr., "How to Raise a Happy Child," *Reader's Digest*, January 1986, 95–98.

Chapter 6 Specific Problems and Disorders of the Young Child

1. Philip Zimbardo, *Shyness, What It is, What to Do About It,* (Reading, Mass.: Addison Wesley, 1977).

2. American Psychiatric Association, *Diagnostic and Statistical Manual of Mental Disorders,* Third Edition, Revised (DSM-III-R) (Washington, D.C.: 1987), 62.

3. *Current Pediatric Diagnosis and Treatment,* 9th ed., C. Henry Kempe, et al. eds., (East Norwalk, Conn.: Appleton and Lange, 1987), 31, 35.

4. Ibid.

5. Ibid.

6. N. Breslau and K. Prabucki, "Siblings of Disabled Children," *Archives of General Psychiatry* 44 (December 1987), 1040–45.

7. Charles Figley, *Helping Traumatized Families* (San Francisco: J. Bass, 1989).

Chapter 7 The Child with Emotional Disorders

1. "U.S. Depressive Disorders Update," a clinical presentation by Martin Keller, M.D., in New Orleans, La., 3 June 1989.

2. Maria Kovacs, "Affective Disorders in Children and Adolescents," *American Psychologist,* vol. 44, no. 2 (January 1989), 209–15.

3. K. L. Lichstein, "Thumbsucking: A Review of Dental and Psychological Variables and Their Implications for Treatment," *JSAS Catalog of Selected Documents in Psychology* 8 (1:1978), 13.

4. Christie Hyde, "The Spoiling Zone," *Parents,* August 1988, 95–98.

5. Ibid.

6. A. Gesell, F. L. Ilg, and L. B. Ames, *The Infant and Child in the Culture of Today* (New York: Harper and Row, 1974).

7. T. F. Anders and P. Weinstein, "Sleep and Its Disorders in Infants and Children: A Review," *Pediatrics* 50 (1972), 312–23.

Chapter 8 Needs of the Grade-School Child

1. Grace W. Weinstein, *Children and Money* (New York: New American Library, 1987).

2. Frances Cogle and G. E. Tasker, "Children and Housework," *Family Relations* 31, 395–99.

3. Elliott Medrich and J. Roizen, *The Serious Business of Growing Up: A Study of Children's Lives Outside School* (Berkeley: University of California Press, 1981).

4. Elin McCoy, "Child Labor," *Parents*, August 1987, 95–101.

5. James P. Comer, "Public Conduct," *Parents*, October 1987, 216.

6. Clarence J. Rowe, *An Outline of Psychiatry*, 9th ed. (Dubuque: William C. Brown Publishers, 1989), 25–26.

Chapter 9 Options of the Grade-School Child

1. Julius and Zelda Segal, "Helping Children Persevere," *Parents*, June 1987, 162.

2. David and Barbara Bjorklund, "Smoothing the Competitive Edge," *Parents*, February 1988, 184.

3. Ibid.

4. David and Barbara Bjorklund, "Getting into the Team Spirit," *Parents*, June 1988, 197.

Chapter 11 Anger and Sibling Rivalry

1. Julius Segal, "I'm So Angry," *Parents*, August 1988, 107–10.

2. Carol Tavris, *Anger: The Misunderstood Emotion* (New York: Simon and Schuster, 1984).

3. G. R. Patterson, Barbara DeBaryshe, and Elizabeth Ramsey, "A Developmental Perspective on Antisocial Behavior," *American Psychologist*, vol. 44, no. 2 (February 1989), 329–35.

4. Ibid.

Chapter 12 Childhood Depression and the Fearful, Anxious Child

1. Martin B. Keller, "Toward DSM-IV and More Accurate Diagnosis of Depression." Paper presented at U.S. Depressive Disorders Update Conference, June 3, 1989, New Orleans, Louisiana.

2. American Psychiatric Association, *Diagnostic and Statistical Manual of Mental Disorders*, Third Edition, Revised (Washington, D.C., 1987).

3. "Toward DSM-IV."

4. Walter Byrd and Paul Warren, *Counseling and Adolescents,* a volume of the Resources for Christian Counseling series to be published in 1990.

5. J. Purg-Antitch, "Psychobiologic Correlate of Major Depressive Disorder in Children and Adolescents," *American Psychiatric Association Annual Review,* L. Grinspoon, ed. (Washington, D.C.: American Psychiatric Press, 1982).

6. "Childhood Fears and Anxieties," *The Harvard Medical School Mental Health Letter,* vol. 5, no. 2 (August 1988), 1–5.

7. Ibid.

Chapter 13 Co-Dependency, Child Abuse, and the Dysfunctional Family

1. Robert Subby, *Lost in the Shuffle, the Co-Dependent Reality* (Pompano Beach, Fla.: Health Communications, 1987), 10, 11.

2. Melody Beattie, *Co-Dependent No More* (New York: Harper and Row-Hazelden Press, 1987).

3. Timmen Cermak, "Diagnosing and Treating Co-Dependence," *Journal of Alcoholism and Addiction* (November-December 1986), 57.

4. Janet Woititz, *Adult Children of Alcoholics* (Pompano Beach, Fla.: Health Communications, 1983), 55–86.

5. See vol. 13 in the Resources for Christian Counseling series, *Counseling for Substance Abuse and Addiction* by Van Cleave, Byrd, and Revell, p. 59, 60.

6. "Highlights of Official Child Neglect and Abuse Reporting" (1987), American Humane Association, 9725 East Hampden Avenue, Denver, CO 80231.

7. Subby, *Lost in the Shuffle.*

Chapter 14 Children with Habit Disorders, Chronic Illnesses, and Handicaps

1. D. Shaffer, "The Clinical Management of Bedwetting in Children," *Handbook of Clinical Assessment of Children and Adolescents* Clarice J. Kestenbaum and Daniel T. Williams, eds. (New York: New York University Press, 1988).

2. Ibid.

3. Ibid.

4. Ibid, 689–706.

5. G. S. Gedden, "The Relationship Between Stimulant Medication and Tics," *Pediatric Annals,* vol. 17, no. 6 (June 1988), 405–08.

6. J. G. Hughes, "The Emotional Impact of Chronic Disease," *American Journal of Diseases of Children* 130 (1976), 1199–1203.

7. See *Counseling the Sick and Terminally Ill* by Gregg R. Albers, vol. 20 in the Resources for Christian Counseling, especially the chapters, "Counseling the Chronically Ill" and "Counseling the Psychiatrically Ill."

Chapter 15 The Child with Attention Deficit Disorder

1. Paul Wender, "An Update on Attention Deficit Disorder," *Currents in Affective Illness,* vol. 7, no. 6 (June 1988), 5–12.

2. Robert Hunt, "Attention Deficit Disorder and Hyperactivity," *Handbook of Clinical Assessment of Children and Adolescents,* vol. 2, Clarice J. Kestenbaum and Daniel T. Williams, eds. (New York: New York University Press, 1988), 519–550.

3. Barry Garfinkel, "Recent Developments in Attention Deficit Disorder," *Psychiatric Annals,* vol. 16, no. 1 (January 1986), 11–15.

4. Ben F. Feingold, *Why Your Child Is Hyperactive* (New York: Random House, 1985).

5. Richard Brunstetter and Larry Silver, "Attention Deficit Disorder," *Comprehensive Textbook of Psychiatry,* Harold Kaplan and Benjamin Sadock, eds. (Baltimore: Williams and Wilkins, 1985), 1690.

6. Garfinkel, "Recent Developments," 16–19.

7. Wender, "An Update."

Chapter 16 Learning Disabilities

1. L. B. Silver, "The Relationship Between Learning Disabilities, Hyperactivity, Distractibility and Behavioral Problems: A Clinical Analysis," *Journal of the American Academy of Child Psychiatry* 20 (1981), 385–97.

2. "The Eye and Learning Disabilities," joint organizational statement of the American Academy of Pediatrics, *Pediatrics* 49 (1972), 454, 455.

3. H. N. Levinson, *A Solution to the Riddle of Dyslexia* (New York: Springer-Verlag New York, Inc., 1981). By the same author: *Smart But Feeling Dumb* (New York: Warner Books, 1984).

Chapter 17 The Spiritual Training of the Child

1. Dan Motet, "Kohlberg's Theory of Moral Development and the Christian Faith," *Journal of Psychology and Theology,* vol. 6, no. 1 (1978), 18–21.

2. David Elkind, "Habits of the Heart," *Parents,* July 1988, 165.

INDEX

Aaron, 213
Abuse: drug, 162–63, 166,
  196–97; physical, 164;
  sexual, 164–65
Acceptance: and worth, 121,
  123; vs. approval, 50
Achievement, 121–23;
  scholastic, 126
Activity level, 7, 22, 24
Adaptability, 7, 22, 24, 32
Adjustment disorders, 92–93
Affection, 16; and anger, 144;
  child's need for, 6, 16;
  resisting, 64
Age: appropriate for tasks, 52
American Academy of
  Opthalmology, 210
American Academy of
  Pediatrics, 210
American Humane
  Association, 164
American Psychiatric
  Association, 16, 89, 91

Anger, 122, 140–46; and
  psychosomatic illness, 141;
  four "stokers" of, 142;
  in ADD child, 200; of
  oppositional child, 71;
  of parent, 23, 43, 55
Antisocial behaviors, 171–77
Anxiety—see fear
Approach/withdrawal, 7,
  22, 25
Approval: vs. acceptance,
  50–51
Assaultiveness, 70
Assignments, 8
Attention deficit disorder, 64,
  189–202; and diet,
  193–94; and hyperactivity,
  191–92; characteristics of,
  190–91; extinguishing
  negative behavior,
  199–200; managing,
  197–99, 201–02;
  medications for, 194–97;

Walter Byrd, M.D.

Walter Byrd is medical director and staff psychiatrist with the Minirth-Meier-Byrd Clinic in Fairfax, Virginia. Formerly he was medical director of the substance abuse program at Memorial Hospital of Garland, Texas. Dr. Byrd, with Stephen Van Cleave, M.D., and Kathy Revell, R.N., C.A.D.A.C., authored *Counseling for Substance Abuse and Addiction*, Volume 12 of the Resources for Christian Counseling series. He is a graduate of the University of Mississippi and the University of Texas Medical School. He and his wife Karen have four children.

Paul A. Warren, M.D.

Paul Warren is the medical director of the Minirth-Meier Clinic Child/Adolescent Division (outpatient) in Richardson, Texas. He also serves as medical director of the clinic's inpatient adolescent and preadolescent unit at Westpark Medical Center in McKinney, Texas. A regular guest on the nationwide call-in radio program, "The Minirth-Meier Clinic," Dr. Warren is certified by the American Board of Pediatrics and a member of the Christian Medical Society. The author of a booklet on attention deficit disorder, he received his medical training at the University of Oklahoma School of Medicine upon graduating from Baylor University. After an internship and residency in pediatrics at the University of Texas Southwestern Medical School/Children's Medical Center, he also completed a fellowship in behavioral pediatrics and adolescent medicine at that institution. He and his wife Vicky have a son, Matthew.